# EDUCATING
# Hispanic and Latino
# STUDENTS

OPENING

DOORS

TO

HOPE,

PROMISE,

AND

POSSIBILITY

## Jaime A. Castellano

**LSi** **LEARNING®**
**SCIENCES**
**INTERNATIONAL**

1400 Centrepark Blvd., Ste 1000
West Palm Beach, FL 33401
717.845.6300
email: pub@learningsciences.com
learningsciences.com

Printed in the United States of America

22 21 20 19 18    1 2 3 4 5


Library of Congress Control Number: 2017961028


Publisher's Cataloging-in-Publication Data
provided by Five Rainbows Cataloging Services

Names: Castellano, Jaime A., author.

Title: Educating Hispanic and Latino students : opening doors to hope, promise, and possibility / Jaime A. Castellano.

Description: West Palm Beach, FL : Learning Sciences, 2018.

Identifiers: LCCN 2017961028 | ISBN 978-1-943920-21-1 (pbk.) | ISBN 978-1-943920-22-8 (ebook)

Subjects: LCSH: Hispanic Americans--Education. | Minority students. | Education--United States. | Teachers--Training of. | BISAC: EDUCATION / Multicultural Education. | EDUCATION / Professional Development.

Classification: LCC LC2670.3.C37 2018 (print) | LCC LC2670.3.C37 (ebook) | DDC 371.829/68--dc23.


Cover design: Free resources used from Vecteezy.com, Open Font License 1.1, and Apache License 2.0.

*This book is dedicated to my mother, Lilia Castellano; to my wife, Lillian; to my eldest son, Jaime, his wife, Natacha, and their daughter, Leila, my granddaughter; to my son Alejandro and his wife, Kelly, and their daughter, Freya, my granddaughter; and to my youngest children, twins Gabriel and Gisell. I also dedicate this book to my sisters, Yolanda, Cynthia, and Olympia, and to my brother, Michael.*

# Table of Contents

# About the Author

 **Dr. Jaime A. Castellano** is a nationally recognized and award-winning principal, award-winning author, scholar, and researcher. He is the author of four books in the field of gifted education and dozens of articles and chapters written for multiple publications. His 2011 book, *Special Populations in Gifted Education: Understanding Our Most Able Students from Diverse Backgrounds*, was awarded the Legacy Award for Outstanding Scholarly Publication in Gifted Education.

Dr. Castellano is recognized as one of our nation's leading authorities in the education of Hispanic/Latino students and in identifying and serving low-income, racially, culturally, and linguistically diverse gifted students with particular expertise on identifying gifted Hispanic/Latino students, African American students, Native American students, English language learners, students from poverty, and preschoolers.

Dr. Castellano has served as a graduate school professor for Arizona State University (gifted education), Florida Atlantic University (educational leadership, special education, and English to speakers of other languages), Lynn University in Florida (educational leadership, special education, English to speakers of other languages), NOVA Southeastern University in Florida (educational leadership, special education), and National Louis University in Illinois (bilingual education, special education).

He served as the co-chair of the Diversity/Equity Committee for the National Association for Gifted Children (NAGC) in 2007 and 2014. He also served on their board of directors from 2008 to 2012. He served on the international board of directors for ASCD from 2006 to 2009. He is currently president of Florida ASCD. He also founded the Gifted Education Special Interest Group (SIG) with the

National Association for Bilingual Education (NABE) and the Professional Interest Community (PIC) on Gifted and Advanced Learners for ASCD.

With more than thirty years as an educator advocating for the educational rights of Hispanic/Latino students, he has served as a teacher of the gifted, assistant principal, and principal supervising gifted education programs; district-level gifted education coordinator and director; and state department of education specialist/expert in the field. He also serves as a reviewer for the *Journal of Advanced Academics* (JAA), *Journal for the Education of the Gifted* (JEG), and *Gifted Child Today* (GCT).

Dr. Castellano is a nationally recognized speaker and professional development trainer and continues to consult with school districts across the country on the education of Hispanic/Latino students and the inclusion of low-income, racially, culturally, and linguistically diverse students in gifted education programming. He currently resides in Lake Worth, Florida, and is the assistant director of the Luciano Martinez Child Development Center and an adjunct professor for Florida Atlantic University in the Department of Exceptional Student Education.

# Acknowledgments

For almost a year, I have spent the vast majority of my weekends in the local public library, written during holiday seasons, and missed a number of family functions—all for the purpose of writing this book, which I think is important and much needed. Therefore, I must first acknowledge my wife, Lillian, and my two youngest children, twins Gabriel and Gisell. Thank you for your patience and understanding.

Thanks go to Dana Lake, Learning Sciences International (LSI) editor extraordinaire, who helped me deliver my message in a more coherent, sensible, and meaningful way. You are a master of your craft, and all of your suggestions were deeply appreciated. To Lesley Bolton, editorial director, for extending the invitation to write for LSI and for never wavering in your support and encouragement. And to Michael Toth, CEO of LSI, for having the vision, leadership, and willingness to listen to new ideas. Your sincerity and wisdom is appreciated.

Thank you also goes to the Palm Beach County Library System, particularly the Lantana Road branch, where I spent hundreds of hours writing. I have seen firsthand the benefits of public libraries and the positive impact they have on a community and its people. I did some of my best work in your location.

In closing, I thank God for blessing me with a passion and gift for writing that I may share with others.

Learning Sciences International would like to thank the following reviewers:

| | |
|---|---|
| Maureen J. Look | Natalie Wester |
| 2010 Wisconsin Teacher of the Year | 2011 Ohio Teacher of the Year |
| Waukesha, Wisconsin | Cleveland, Ohio |

# Preface

The education of Hispanic/Latino students, from prekindergarten to graduate school, is of paramount importance to the future of the United States. I am an experienced and award-winning educator, principal, author, researcher, and scholar who identifies with the issues and challenges related to educating this important group of students who continue to lag behind educationally due to a complexity of factors. One of the driving principles of this book is that Hispanic/Latino students are vital linguistic, economic, and social resources to our society in an increasingly globalized and interdependent world. Thus, a fundamental belief of this book is that given proper support, every student has the chance for a successful and meaningful future. In addition, if we empower our Hispanic/Latino parents and families, I believe they will become a nationwide driving force for creating more equitable and responsive school environments for their children.

I am a lifelong educator of Mexican American descent from one of Chicago's southside Mexican barrios, one of the lucky ones who escaped the poverty, abuse, neglect, and violence of my dysfunctional community. For me, it was leave or become a product of my environment—an environment rooted in poverty, gangs, drugs, incarceration, and death. At seventeen years of age, I chose to leave my barrio to attend a state university. There was no other option. In my youth I attended the Chicago Public Schools (W. K. Sullivan Elementary School and James H. Bowen High School) and the university system of Illinois (Northern Illinois University and Chicago State University). Education was the game changer for me. It opened doors that I did not even know existed at the time.

During my career as a public school teacher, school-based administrator, and district-level leader, I have worked primarily with low-income racially, culturally, and linguistically diverse groups of students, with particular experience working with, and advocating for, Hispanic/Latino students from those in special education to those identified as gifted, advanced, and high-ability and from the poorest to the wealthiest. I have worked with Hispanic/Latino students from urban, rural, and suburban communities. I saw firsthand how other educators and colleagues demeaned, ridiculed, and had lower expectations for these students, thus perpetuating racism, discrimination, and inequity. And I often wondered if this was by choice or due to ignorance. Those of us who had hope, high expectations, and inspiration were greatly outnumbered.

My purpose for writing this book is personal. I want to share my experiences, thoughts, and ideas with other educators from across the country who serve Hispanic/Latino students. This book delivers a plethora of statistical data, adds to the research on this population of students, and offers teachers and administrators a number of strategies that can positively impact the teaching and learning experience through curriculum, instruction, and assessment. Furthermore, I hope that this book allows students, parents and families, teachers, administrators, researchers and scholars, school boards, legislators, and policymakers to continue their advocacy; that hope remains eternal; and that there is still time to turn the tide of mediocrity in how we educate this population of students who are an untapped national resource and treasure.

Hispanic/Latino students now represent the largest ethnic group being educated in our public school system, yet few pieces of literature are available to support the development of these special learners. This book represents a vision to help our nation become more proactive in addressing the needs of this important group of students. It is designed to educate, inform, and empower. Its intent is to disseminate the relevant, practical, and culturally responsive information and data that educators, parents, and families need in providing these students with every opportunity to actualize and demonstrate what they know and are able to do.

In the end, my primary hope is that this book will make a difference for a group of students who historically have been disenfranchised, neglected, and often prevented from exercising their individual and collective talent and potential.

# Introduction

The enrollment of Hispanic/Latino students in our nation's schools is outpacing the readiness and infrastructure required to both effectively educate them and prepare them for a successful future. The most recent example is the dramatic and well-documented immigration of unaccompanied school-aged children from Central and South America, some fifty thousand strong, that has impacted our schools since 2014. The *KIDS COUNT Data Book* by the Annie E. Casey Foundation (2016) reports that there are 17.6 million Latino children in the United States, representing 25 percent of the country's child population. Combining the continued influx of children from Central and South America and the steady flow of immigrant children from Mexico, deduction tells us this number is now well over 18 million. The *KIDS COUNT Data Book* goes on to document that the education of Latino students is cause for deep concern, with the greatest concern tied to those primarily located in the Mid-South and Southwestern regions of the United States.

In a review of the research by the Annie E. Casey Foundation (2016), National Center for Education Statistics (2016a), the United States Department of Education (2010), its Office for Civil Rights (2016), the National Assessment of Educational Progress (NAEP) (2016), the United States Census Bureau (2016), Child Trends Data Bank (2016), Child Trends Hispanic Institute (2017), and ACT and Excelencia in Education (2016), among other sources, I am saddened by what I read. Each, through its own unique perspective and data set, tells us we have a long road ahead of us as the "browning of America" continues to touch every facet of our educational system. Current data and research paint a bleak picture. Rather than shy away from these facts or let them discourage us as educators, we must use them as a motivating force to galvanize parents, teachers, administrators, policymakers, elected officials, and other stakeholder groups. We must band together at the local, state, and national levels to make the equal education of all our children a priority.

## Status and Trends in the Education of Hispanic/Latino Students

To get to where we're going, we must understand where we are. In terms of status, as a nation, we have categorically failed our Hispanic/Latino students. Despite scattered reports that demonstrate progress has been made, Hispanic/Latino students remain in the bottom 25 percent as a national cohort across nearly all reports documenting academic achievement. This status has developed into a trend now that this subgroup of students has longitudinally been linked to the lowest-achieving ethnic groups for at least the past thirty years. This book will explore some of the contributing factors to the current state of our education system and what changes we must make now if we want a better future.

## The Promise of Equity and Excellence in Education Opportunities

Educational excellence is inextricably linked to educational equity. Matters of equity must continue to drive our national conversations and conscience so that all children will be given the opportunity to develop to their maximum potential. If the preponderance of our Hispanic/Latino students are Spanish-speakers, does educational excellence lie in the form of bilingual education, particularly dual-language immersion programs that honor one's language, culture, and heritage? Allowing students to access a curriculum through their heritage language makes sense and provides a reliable and valid platform for them to demonstrate what they know and are able to do.

Teachers, principals, and other instructional and educational leaders can further the promise of educational excellence by working together and completing the professional development needed to apply principles of equity and cultural competency and to create a culturally responsive classroom environment. Educational excellence and opportunity require us to take a look at the whole child. While the litmus test for success is often grounded in academic achievement and test scores, we are now learning about the importance of the social and emotional growth of all students and its link to long-term success and productivity. Through the administration of interest inventories and in honest, coherent conversations about how each student learns best, teachers develop practices and procedures that honor strength-based programming. In turn, equity, access, and opportunity are enhanced.

## Nomenclature

The labeling of students in our nation's schools is used for funding purposes, program placement, and demographic descriptions, among other reasons. Diaz (2002) notes that defining and making choices in labeling people and their attributes is a difficult process due to the complexity of understanding the interconnections among the terms. Yet, this is a standard practice of our American education institutions.

In this book, both *Hispanic* and *Latino* are used, depending on the research cited. For example, the Annie E. Casey Foundation uses the term *Latino*, which was defined by the Office of Management and Budget (OMB) for use by federal statistical agencies. People who use this category (label) can be of any racial group and include people from Mexico, Central and South America, and other Spanish-speaking countries. The term *Latino* is also used by the Civil Rights Project / Proyecto Derechos Civiles at the University of California, Los Angeles, whereas the United States Census Bureau and the United States Office of Juvenile Justice and Delinquency Prevention use the term *Hispanic*.

## Themes and Topics

No one can refute the existing challenges we face in educating Hispanic/Latino students in the United States. The problems are all too real and easily documented through local, state, national, and international achievement data. This book will focus on four of the most complex issues and their implications: immigration, poverty, identity, and bias.

Within these issues is the common theme of communication and collaboration among and between important stakeholder groups: parents and families, the school, the school district, and the local community. As the reader will discover, this book includes a diversity of perspectives unique to where the students are in the American education hierarchy.

Each solution or strategy in this book attempts to achieve equity, access, and opportunity for all students. Equity is the right to fair and unbiased instruction, access is the right to engage in all aspects of the curriculum, and opportunity is the right to strive for success and a brighter future.

## Organization of the Book

This book is divided into four complex issues and their implications for the education of Hispanic/Latino students. Each chapter will provide topical, practical, and culturally relevant strategies for parents, teachers, administrators, and other educational and instructional staff to consider.

Chapter 1 addresses the realities of immigration, both legal and illegal. The stress of living in a sometimes openly hostile country can combine with the trauma many undocumented Hispanic/Latino students suffer crossing the border and being separated from family. The educational gaps these students contend with further complicate their academic needs. This chapter identifies warning signs teachers can look for in students needing more comprehensive emotional and academic support, in addition to techniques for making the classroom a welcoming and safe place for all students.

Chapter 2 addresses the poverty rate for Hispanic/Latino students—more than double that of white students. High poverty levels mean Hispanic/Latino students are more likely to attend Title I schools, more likely to work while going to school, and more likely to live in areas with few public resources. This chapter outlines constructive programs to provide the structure these students may not have at home and explores how educators can incorporate a whole-student approach into their lessons.

Chapter 3 addresses the struggles Hispanic/Latino students have in shaping their personal identities. The balance of obligations to school, community, and family requires complex and sometimes contradictory behaviors, including the use of different languages. As the largest minority group in American schools, Hispanic/Latino students are often treated as one homogeneous group—in reality, these students hail from nineteen different countries and one territory. This chapter details how to engage with Hispanic/Latino culture in the classroom without painting all students with a single brush and provides methods to involve English language learners in school effectively.

Chapter 4 addresses the taboo topic of teacher bias. The role of unconscious bias cannot be mitigated until it is appropriately identified and treated. Rather than shy away from reality, this chapter outlines practical techniques educators can utilize to overcome their own internal biases that may influence how Hispanic/Latino students perform in school.

CHAPTER 1

# Adverse Life Experiences

When asked about how her Hispanic ethnicity has affected her academic development and how it has influenced her aspirations, Sara responds, "My family and I are immigrants. We moved from Mexico to the United States when I was seven. We are a family of five, with my father being the only one who works. Neither of my parents speaks English. Over the years, I have come to learn the language, which has helped me do well in school. Our inability to speak English when we first arrived to the United States was a huge obstacle. In this country, we need to know the language; it is spoken everywhere. It was difficult to speak to the people around us. This affected my grades when we first arrived because I didn't understand the homework or the activities we would do in class. Although it was a difficult stage for me, it only made me work harder to learn the language enough so that I would not have to depend on someone to interpret for me or my parents."

Sara goes on to say, "Sometimes I feel like people tend to underestimate my abilities because I am Hispanic. This only motivates me to work harder and embrace my ethnicity even more—to prove to those who doubt me that being Hispanic does not determine what I am capable of or limit my possibilities. I want to go to college and become a successful person whom Hispanics can be proud of. I know that with hard work and dedication I will be able to accomplish whatever I want, as long as I keep my goal in mind."

"My goal was to graduate and be in the top ten of my high school graduating class. I met that goal. Being part of the International Baccalaureate (IB) program helped me stay busy and focused in school. Although IB is a great program, it was very hard for me to get things done because of the limited resources in my school. I feel like that because this is a minority school we are often overlooked in the things we need. Sometimes to actually learn certain lessons, I had to teach myself and find the materials I needed online. I'm grateful for this now because

Continued →

not only did it teach me to be independent, but I also became a better critical thinker and problem solver."

Sara attended a rural Title I high school in a South Florida area that is agricultural, remote, and lacks the fundamental resources and services that a healthy community requires. Its isolation informs a level of abject poverty where 100 percent of the students receive a free or reduced-priced lunch. Nonetheless, Sara has shown the resiliency and perseverance that empowers, allowing her to move forward with her plans to attend college.

One of Sara's teachers writes that she is an amazing young woman professionally, academically, and personally. "She is continually helping and supporting a multitude of students as well as other teachers and staff members. She displays exceptional knowledge, critical thinking skills, communication skills, and leadership abilities. It became evident very early in my interactions with her that she is a kind, caring, and compassionate individual. She strives to do her best." A local attorney, who serves as one of her mentors, adds, "She has revealed her leadership abilities by her eagerness to serve. There is no challenge too big or too small for her to take on, and she has shown a consistent willingness to volunteer her assistance with any project we undertake, in whatever capacity may be required. She is unwavering in her commitment to the group. She is fully bilingual and ready to make a difference in the world."

Sara is a survivor. She demonstrates the characteristics required of today's successful students. To come from a community where abject poverty is the norm, and that is often forgotten, and to excel academically, socially, and emotionally like she has makes her the kind of individual who can effectively navigate the many challenges that life often puts in our way. She is also resolute in her desire to be a role model for her younger siblings and other Hispanic students of her rural community.

Why did I choose to write *Educating Hispanic and Latino Students* and not *Educating Historically Disadvantaged Students*? While those books would certainly overlap in places, the Hispanic/Latino story is uniquely written in the United States. In art, music, movies, and politics we experience the widest range of contradictory portrayals: the loving abuela and the angry gang member; the cowboy and the Casanova; the Aztec king and the migrant worker. No aspect of how the Hispanic/Latino diaspora is portrayed is more complicated than the role of immigration: According to the United States Department of Education's 2017 report titled *Status and Trends in the Education of Racial and Ethnic Groups*, while 94 percent of the Hispanic student population under the age of eighteen were born in the United States in 2014, 6 percent of Hispanic/Latino students were not and are documented as immigrants; more than half (55 percent) of all first- and second-generation immigrant children were of Hispanic origin in 2014, according to Child Trends Data Bank (2014). This information and data helps reinforce the intra-ethnic diversity among Hispanic and Latino students, and how immigration continues to be part of the narrative that must be told, particulary when it comes to how to educate this unique group of students. The Lucille Packard Foundation for Children's Health (2015) states that Hispanic/Latino students make up 25.6 percent of all public school enrollment in the United States. Furthermore, the Pew Research Center (2016) documents that despite slowing growth rates, Latinos still accounted for more than half (54 percent) of the total US population growth from 2000 to 2014. All this is to say a significant portion of the students in our public schools are, or are the children of, immigrants.

How these students engage with immigration is hugely significant to how they engage with their education. Children born to undocumented immigrants in the United States face unique challenges in attaining resources and stability that other students do not, and students who are themselves undocumented have even higher hurdles to overcome. No human being can be "illegal," but the careless rhetoric of teachers, legislatures, and other people in power that makes students feel illegal is not something that is easily brushed off. Part of the problem is that the schools responsible for educating these students fail to take the trauma of being "illegal" into consideration. These students may have come here as unaccompanied minors, escaping from horrible circumstances. They are often the victims or witnesses of crime and dealing with toxic stress. They may have gaps in their education that are difficult to overcome without intervention. These students and their families should be able to expect an education of the same quality as that of their white, black, and Asian peers and that is free from political maneuvering—the neutral ground of schools should serve as community pillars, a safe space. This chapter explores these issues and how schools activating greater parental engagement can be the solution for many of them.

## Unaccompanied Minors

Over the past few years, educators have realized that students are arriving to school having witnessed or been a part of some traumatic event that has left them socially and emotionally vulnerable. One such group is the unaccompanied minors from Central America and Mexico. The Migration Policy Institute (2015a) documents that more than 102,000 unaccompanied children from Central America and Mexico were apprehended at the US-Mexico border by US Customs and Border Protection from the start of fiscal year (FY) 2014 through August 31, 2015. That's a difficult number to conceptualize—over 100,000 is about the total population of Boulder, Colorado—arriving in the United States in less than two years. In four years, the number becomes bigger than the population of Montgomery, Alabama; in six years, the number of unaccompanied minors is equivalent to the population of Pittsburgh, Pennsylvania. By any reckoning, this is an overwhelming movement of children across dangerous terrain. They face the environmental danger of great swaths of desert and the personal danger of predatory adults, all without the protection of their parents. From the beginning of FY 2014 through August 31, 2015, 77,194 unaccompanied minors were released by the Office of Refugee Resettlement (ORR) into communities throughout the United States. These minors are entitled to a public education. For school districts and communities to better serve these children, it is essential to understand where they have come from, why they have left, and the challenges they face in their new home.

The majority of unaccompanied children are from the Northern Triangle countries of El Salvador, Guatemala, and Honduras, which accounted for more than 76,000 of the 102,000 child immigrants mentioned previously. While current agreements between the United States and Mexico allow for most Mexican children caught to be returned to their homes, US law provides for different treatment of unaccompanied minors from noncontiguous countries. These children may qualify for asylum, indicating the United States recognizes they are unable to return to their homes for fear of persecution. There are eighteen Spanish-speaking countries and one territory in Latin America and the Caribbean from which these children emigrate, each with its own risks; they may have crossed oceans, trekked through deserts, cut through jungle, and braved manipulative coyotes or human traffickers on their own. In August of 2017, sixteen-year-old Brandon Martinez was one of dozens of undocumented immigrants smuggled into the United States in an unventilated truck. Tickets for the ride cost thousands of dollars for what the smugglers promised would be a comfortable and easy journey. Without air-conditioning in the summer heat and with only one small hole to take turns breathing through, Brandon watched as ten people died in the crossing. He and several other passengers were fortunately admitted to a hospital in time for treatment after being found.

For unaccompanied minors to make the decision to journey from their homes and the lives they knew to a brand-new country and the tenuous idea of a new life, there must be significantly motivating factors. According to Child Trends (2016), through the first six months of FY 2016, 27,754 unaccompanied children were apprehended at the southwest border. Border patrol officials predicted that in FY 2017, 75,000 would cross the US-Mexico border by themselves.

A combination of push and pull factors influences these thousands of children. The most common push factor for fleeing their home countries is the fear of violence, particularly by gangs. Child Trends (2016) also reports that most (68 percent in FY 2015) unaccompanied children are older teens (fifteen to seventeen), but one in six (17 percent) is under thirteen. The Office of the United Nations High Commissioner for Refugees interviewed more than four hundred children, ages twelve to seventeen, from Mexico and the Northern Triangle who arrived during or after October 2011. The researchers found that 58 percent had been forced to emigrate because of harm they suffered or threats they faced. Forty-eight percent had been affected personally by organized violence; 22 percent were victims of domestic abuse; and 11 percent reported experiencing or fearing violence both at home and in the community. The most common pull factor is to be reunited with parents or other family members. This is what drove Brandon to agree to the dangerous truck crossing—he was attempting to reunite with his father, who had emigrated a year earlier. They were able to finally meet again in the hospital Brandon was taken to for treatment.

For all the children caught by US Customs and Border Protection, there are many more who enter the United States and attempt to navigate a new life here without the intervention of government refugee assistance. The common thread between the push and pull factors of illegal immigration is the need to resolve trauma—either by escaping abuse or by reuniting with family. For whatever reason, thousands of minors cross the border every year through dangerous methods because they cannot wait for the wheels of US immigration policy to turn. It then falls to the communities they settle in to help them adjust. The most visible and immediate impact of this new child population is felt by local school districts, which are serving growing volumes of new students, often with little time to prepare. These children have mostly been placed in states with large Central American immigrant communities: California, Texas, Florida, Virginia, Maryland, and New York. The child immigrants have an array of particular needs, among them social and emotional needs, and school districts have had to balance addressing these needs along with those of other students, within resource limitations.

Anecdotal reports suggest school districts are reacting in significantly different ways. Some are creating service programs that address particular needs, while others have exercised policies that make school enrollment more difficult. These students, welcomed or not, are now part of a local community and have the right to attend the local public school. It would behoove local school districts to embrace this reality and promote inclusionary strategies such as cross-cultural communication and understanding, an attention to serving the whole child, and to embrace the diversity the students represent. This is not to say the care of this unique subgroup of Hispanic/Latino students will be easy if only we can open our minds and hearts; that is the critical first step but not the end of the discussion. The economic realities of their care cannot be ignored. Congressional appropriations for FY 2015 provided an additional $14 million for local education agencies to provide services targeted specifically to unaccompanied minors in thirty-five states that received significant numbers of arrivals. Based on the assumption that about 60,000 unaccompanied child immigrants have been placed in US schools since the start of FY 2014, this grant amounts to about $233 per student, leaving most of the cost to be borne by the local school district. A sustainable method of low-cost, personalized intervention is parental involvement, which will be further explored in the last section of this chapter.

It takes an unforgivable lack of empathy to expect undocumented and unaccompanied minors to easily "move on" from their experiences. Though some students may be able to compartmentalize and cope more effectively than others, most unaccompanied children share one or more traumatic experiences: separation from parents and other family members; exposure to violence; uprooting from familiar contexts of language, community, and culture; homelessness and housing instability; prejudice and discrimination on the basis of color, religion, or language; poor physical and mental health; interrupted schooling; economic hardships; lack of access to formal and informal social supports; and anxiety for their future. In Brandon's case, he has been reunited with his father and is under the protection of the US government while charges are brought against the human traffickers. For other minors, it is critical that the experience of trauma is buffered by supportive adults—this includes all stakeholder groups but most importantly the family and teachers. Without a support system, trauma can lead to toxic stress.

## Toxic Stress

Child Trends (2016) reports that toxic stress harms children's development. Its effects reach into the brain's structure and function, impairing cognitive, social, and emotional skills; compromising health; and contributing to risk for disease and early death. Although many experiences can lead to toxic stress, the most significant of these for the children who are the focus here involve separation from parents and the experience of violence, either as a direct victim or as a witness. The causes of toxic stress, its effects on Hispanic/Latino learners, and the role of local school districts are further explored in this section.

Factors that have a negative social-emotional impact on students include abuse and neglect, violence, gangs, drugs, alcoholism, homelessness, and poverty, among others. Hispanic/Latino students who are witnesses to the events listed in the previous sentence suffer psychologically. Students who are victims may be scarred forever. According to Child Trends (2016) and their document titled *Moving beyond Trauma: Child Migrants and Refugees in the United States*, more than 127,000 children, with or without their parents, sought refuge in the United States in 2016. "Classified according to a number of legal designations, these children share a common experience of trauma, which often accompanies them on their journey to this country and for months or years after they arrive." As many as 90,000 will arrive without legal status, first apprehended by the border patrol, then subjected to a chain of administrative procedures that offer few protections and may include detention for prolonged periods. This presents a great many hazards to their well-being, including re-traumatization. "All of these children have significant needs in the areas of family stability, health, education, and economic security." Separation from parents and other family members often takes a double toll on children, "since reunifications can also be highly stressful. Serious mental health problems are prevalent among this population, largely as a result of trauma or anxiety about further separations."

The level of toxic stress one is exposed to early in life, particularly when the brain is developing, impacts learning and achievement, both academically and socially. Children suffering from posttraumatic stress disorder (PTSD) may be impulsive or aggressive and may even reenact traumatic experiences in their play. Feelings of sadness and anger may be reccurring. Children suffering from depression may have trouble sleeping, feelings of worthlessness, and poor eating habits. These cognitive and behavioral changes serve to distance traumatized children from their peers, leading to further feelings of abandonment and isolation. They also make classroom learning difficult; often, learning will be the last priority for these vulnerable youths. Any combination of these mental health issues confounds an already complex educational process. Some of our colleagues may believe that these are simply more excuses for why Hispanic/Latino students do less well in school. Others would argue that you cannot separate these realities from the students we serve and that it is our collective responsibility to accommodate their needs by ensuring that educating the whole child is the school's and district's priority.

Toxic stress is real for tens of thousands of children—for those born and raised in the United States and for those who reach the United States as unaccompanied immigrants. Because education is a fundamental right, schools must contend with these children daily. Child Trends (2016) also reports that children often bring a history of interrupted schooling, or none at all, and face a number of challenges adapting to our education system. Financial circumstances for their families are typically precarious and subject to severe shocks when adult earners are suddenly removed. Like other countries, the United States faces challenges integrating these young newcomers, but our ability to do so will enhance our human, economic, and cultural capital.

For these students, counseling is almost always a benefit. Children in the country illegally or the children of undocumented immigrants may not have the same access to counseling services and government help as their naturalized peers. It is in situations like this when schools must step forward to care for all their students. School counselors partnering with the community's social and mental health services and coordinating with parents is a critical bridge in providing traumatized children with the help they may otherwise have to survive without.

Each month, the Luciano Martinez Child Development Center in West Palm Beach, Florida, conducts a parent meeting. The school's mental health coordinator is present in every meeting. Part of the coordinator's allocated time is given to social service or mental health providers from the community to inform parents of the services available to them. This partnership directly links parents and families to service providers. In the past, parents have commented that if it were not for the parent meetings, they would be unaware of what community-based services were available to them. In addition, multiple social service and mental health providers participate in the school's information fair held in the spring of each year. Materials and information are provided in English and Spanish. These activities proactively form a mental health network among the school, community, and parents and families. It is such relationships among school, community, and family with a focus on the child's whole well-being that create the strongest chances for success. At minimum, immigrant children's social and emotional psyche must be addressed in order to prevent serious mental health problems in the future.

## Educational Gaps

From high school through undergrad, Hispanic/Latino students lag behind their African American and white peer groups in completing school (table 1.1). The effects of both legal and illegal immigration have a multigenerational influence on the education achievement levels of Hispanic/Latino students, most critically in the form of educational gaps. Elementary, middle, and high schools that service these children are challenged in how to best serve them while also balancing the expectation of using age- and/or grade-level-appropriate standards, curriculum, instruction, and assessment practices. To better understand this aspect of Hispanic/Latino education, we will look at the effects of immigration on the education achievement levels of three different groups: immigrant children, children of immigrants, and second-generation citizens.

Table 1.1: Level of Education Completed by Young Adults, Ages Twenty-Five to Twenty-Nine, 2015

|  | Hispanic | Black | White |
|---|---|---|---|
| High School or More | 77% | 92% | 95% |
| Some College or More | 46% | 58% | 72% |
| Bachelor's Degree or Higher | 16% | 21% | 43% |

Educational gaps appear in the educational experiences of both documented and undocumented immigrant children. Both types of immigrants may be coming from areas with very poor schooling and few resources. In rural areas, minors may be expected to enter the workforce to help support the family after a certain age. For minors who enter the country illegally, even those coming from wealthier cities who had access to early schooling, educational gaps arise during the sometimes months-long journey to cross the border. When these children enter the US education system, they are very likely to be English language learners (ELLs), missing some or all of the fundamental lessons further education is built on. The challenge of settling into a new home in a new country with a new language is thus further compounded by struggles to keep up with their peers in school.

The second group, children of immigrants, experience educational gaps physically and emotionally. Physically, Hispanic/Latino children are less likely to be enrolled in early childhood education programs than their peers. They are more often kept at home or with a relative and are less likely to be exposed to critical language- and math-building skills. As a result, Hispanic/Latino children start kindergarten already behind their peers. Emotionally, Hispanic/Latino children experience educational gaps in the form of limited parental education achievement. In 2014, the Child Trends Hispanic Institute reported that only 16 percent of Hispanic young adults (ages twenty-five to twenty-nine) completed postsecondary degrees in 2013, as compared to blacks (19.9 percent) and whites (39.2 percent). The number of Hispanics with a high school diploma is reported to be at about 73 percent. Less educated parents may not be able to provide their children with the kind of experiences needed to be prepared for kindergarten, or school in general, and do not provide these students with an education role model.

For second-generation citizens and beyond, educational gaps appear as they do for other disadvantaged populations: low expectations and lack of resources. According to Gandara (2005), high-performing students tend to come from higher-income and higher-educated families. Students from such backgrounds often have a multitude of financial and educational resources at their disposal. However, among economically disadvantaged groups, as well as groups for whom racial, ethnic, and linguistic discrimination remains a reality, the landscape may be very different. Unlike other high-achieving students, Hispanics/Latinos who demonstrate high academic ability and obtain college degrees—especially those of Mexican and Puerto Rican ancestry—are not as likely to come from economically and educationally advantaged backgrounds. Perseverance, grit, resiliency, and higher levels of intelligence are characteristics typically associated with Hispanic/Latino students and other racially, culturally, and linguistically diverse groups of students who demonstrate a desire to pursue advanced degrees at the master and doctorate levels.

It is vital that educators take the time to encourage Hispanic/Latino students to succeed in the classroom. The Child Trends Data Bank (2016) reports that young adults who have completed higher levels of education are more likely to achieve economic success than those who have not. In addition to qualifying one for a broader range of jobs, completing more years of education also protects against unemployment. Further, higher levels of education attainment often lead to higher wages and income. In 2015, Americans with bachelor's degrees or higher earned a median income that was more than 73 percent higher than that of their peers with only a high school diploma. Adults with higher levels of education also report having better health and high levels of socioemotional well-being. They are also less likely to divorce or be incarcerated. In 2015, among young adults ages twenty-five to twenty-nine, the percentage of whites who had attained at least a bachelor's degree (43 percent) was 2.5 times that of Hispanics

(16 percent) (Child Trends Data Bank, 2016). Hispanic students who pursue a higher education put themselves in a position to become more financially secure. Simply put, the more education one has, the more income one has the potential to earn. The US Bureau of Labor Statistics (2016) and the US Census Bureau (2016) clearly show a correlation between education and income (table 1.2).

Table 1.2: Educational Attainment of Hispanic Population Twenty-Five Years and Over, 2015

| High School Graduate | Some College, No Degree | Associate's: Occupational | Associate's: Academic | Bachelor's Degree | Master's Degree | Professional Degree | Doctoral Degree |
|---|---|---|---|---|---|---|---|
| 9,257,000 | 4,397,000 | 983,000 | 1,242,000 | 3,338,000 | 1,085,000 | 209,000 | 169,000 |
| **2015: Median Annual Wage: Occupational Employment Statistics Program:** | | | | | | | |
| High School Diploma or Equivalent | Some College, No Degree | Postsecondary Non-degree: | Associate's Degree | Bachelor's Degree | Master's Degree | Doctoral or Professional Degree | |
| $36,210 | $33,870 | $35,660 | $50,230 | $70,400 | $66,420 | $100,490 | |

Schooling is an intervention that pays dividends reflected in intelligence scores. Ceci and Williams (1997) amassed evidence that schooling and intelligence contribute to each other and that both affect later income. High intelligence is conducive to prolonged schooling. But it is also true that intelligence scores tend to rise during the school year and drop over the summer months. Summer break is the only educational gap most American-born, wealthier students ever have to deal with. As teachers, we complain about summer brain drain on our students; we need to recognize the effects of other educational gaps in Hispanic/Latino students with compassion rather than exasperation. It takes time and emotional investment to fill all the educational gaps Hispanic/Latino children experience as a result of their or their parents' choice to begin a new life in the United States. Rather than wash our hands of these students and count them as a loss, it is critical that we (all stakeholders) recognize the challenges these students must overcome just to break even academically. If they are willing to learn, we must be willing to teach. By filling the gaps and encouraging students to reach higher levels of learning, we can positively influence the quality of life for not only them but also their children and grandchildren.

## Neutral Ground

In its *KIDS COUNT Data Book*, the Annie E. Casey Foundation (2016) states that when communities have strong institutions and resources to provide safety, good schools, and quality support services, families and their children are more likely to thrive. For some parents, enrolling in an adult education program through the district or local community college may be the best beginning. For others, being recruited into a district leadership team of parents allows them to advocate for all students, not just their own. And still for other parents and families, identifying a sensitive and empathetic Spanish/English-speaking mentor may be the best course of action to allay their fears. That is the best-case scenario, but it exists in very few of the communities Hispanic/Latino families are settled into as refugees or choose to move to. In reality, the high poverty levels of Hispanic/Latino immigrants and lack of community resources means these families are less likely to thrive and more likely to just survive. Hispanic/Latino families who are undocumented are often the most at risk and the least likely to seek government assistance. Fear of deportation or fracturing of the family drives many of these parents to cope with their situation on their own, while pride and similarly difficult situations can make reaching out to neighbors difficult. It is within this liminal space of need and isolation that the neutral power of schools can have the greatest impact.

In many Hispanic/Latino communities, the schools serve as a hub for participation and an opportunity for outreach that can take many forms: from adult English as a second language (ESL) and general equivalency diploma (GED) classes to programs promoting proper nutrition and mental health services and from learning how to engage with a child's teachers and the importance of attendance to accessing additional resources like the local public library and social service agencies and learning about parental rights and responsibilities. Schools exist, and should exist, independent of government immigration policy. As such, schools may consider the following strategies to address government immigration policy, while staying politically neutral.

- Allow students to share experiences/feelings verbally, in writing, or through various art forms.
- Identify and share local community resources with parents and families.
- Implement classroom-based activities that allow students to relax and de-stress (yoga, breathing exercises, stress balls, movement activities, etc.).
- Invite guest speakers to share their stories with students.
- Provide parents and families with space to form support groups for each other.

Schools improve the quality of life and chance for success of all their students—undocumented or naturalized, the first generation of their family born here or the hundredth. Making this clear to the community your school serves is vital to the long-term success of Hispanic/Latino students. Schools that engage the communities they serve have greater success in their communication and collaboration. The goal is to help the child's family develop the knowledge, competence, confidence, and comfort in areas related to their child's development, education, and support. When working with Hispanic/Latino parents and families, the goal from the very beginning is to enhance family functioning, and while individualized support plans are child-focused, the design and implementation should be family-centered. Table 1.3 identifies four tiers of parent involvement that characterize the level of school effort and commitment. Which tier best reflects your school's effort and commitment? Each tier is progressive.

**Table 1.3: Hispanic Parents and Families: Levels of Engagement**

| Level 4 | ▸ School has a designated parent liaison position. <br> ▸ School engages in home visits to build relationships. <br> ▸ School has dedicated parent seats on key decision-making committees. <br> ▸ School offers parenting classes and adult education. <br> ▸ School has a designated parent center. <br> ▸ School engages individual parents/families based on need. |
|---|---|
| Level 3 | ▸ School provides parents with educational resources and materials for home. <br> ▸ School provides parents with electronic access to student attendance, grades, teachers, and other school personnel. <br> ▸ School signage is also in Spanish. <br> ▸ School has front office personnel who speak Spanish. |
| Level 2 | ▸ School provides child care so parents and families can attend events. <br> ▸ School provides refreshments, snacks, or meals as an incentive to attend school events. <br> ▸ School communicates in the heritage language of the families and communities it serves. |
| Level 1 | ▸ School seeks parent volunteers. <br> ▸ School invites parents and families to attend open house, curriculum night, and parent-teacher conferences. |

## Parental Involvement

Unaccompanied minors making dangerous border crossings alone, the effects of toxic stress as a result of untreated trauma, gaps in critical periods of a student's education, and a lack of money on federal, state, and local levels to do much of anything about it—how are we as educators expected to provide personalized, active care for every single one of these vulnerable students? The task seems unsurmountable without a serious restructuring of policy priorities, and while that would certainly make things much easier, there is an invaluable resource schools are only just now beginning to access: parental involvement. Culturally, the reverence that many Hispanic/Latino parents and families have toward their children's school and teachers prevents them from asserting themselves in the education process. They trust that teachers will do the right thing by their children and that they should not question that authority. Our collective responsibility to Hispanic/Latino families is to provide them with the tools to help their children succeed—from the first generation to the hundredth. In our current system, school districts cannot balance the many needs of immigrant and first-generation students with the many needs of other student populations alone.

Building effective bridges of communication among districts, teachers, parents, and the local community—bringing all stakeholder groups together in a structured, effective way—is the solution. By providing opportunities that allow Hispanic/Latino families to engage and interact with other parents, families, and school personnel, we are providing the opportunity for education and empowerment. While we may complain about the current state of "helicopter parenting," the truth is that family should be a child's first advocate. The purpose of this section is to identify and apply research and practices that are responsive to the unique needs of collaborating with Hispanic/Latino parents and families—to teach them how to be advocates for their child. These strategies are effective for whomever the student's guardian is; even unaccompanied minors who have not been reunited with their parents will be in the care of relatives or foster families educators must engage in the student's educational success.

To begin this engagement, it is important to dismiss several assumptions an educator may have about Hispanic/Latino parental involvement. How would you respond to the following statements?

- Present economic conditions require many of our Hispanic/Latino parents to work two, sometimes three jobs to make ends meet. This, in part, is why they do not attend school-sponsored events.

- A fear of immigration and deportation and/or a lack of trust in the school and its leaders is why, in part, Hispanic/Latino parents do not attend school-sponsored events.

- The climate of the school is unwelcoming. It is as if they don't want us to be in their school. They don't even communicate with us in our language, Spanish. We never see them, the teachers and principal, in our communities.

- I do not attend school-sponsored events because the school and teachers know how to teach and know more about educating children than I do. I trust and respect them. I will not challenge their authority or question what they do.

Often the reasons we assume to explain behaviors are far more negative than the reality of a situation. Educators who disparage Hispanic/Latino parental involvement may be lacking in empathy for the difficult position these families are in. What I propose for these teachers is to ask themselves a final question: "Is my attitude constructive to my student's learning?" If we approach parental involvement with the idea of failure already in place, then what we create is a self-fulfilling prophecy. To get parents to engage, teachers must be willing to engage. For extensive techniques on resetting your perspective, see Raise the Floor and Ceiling in chapter 4.

The simplest way to activate Hispanic/Latino parental engagement is to utilize both English and Spanish in all communications. Whether a Hispanic/Latino family lives in New Hampshire or Vermont or New Mexico or Texas, Castellano (2016) writes, schools and districts that educate Hispanic/Latino students have a duty and responsibility to effectively communicate with their constituents in the language of the families and communities they serve. It takes time to translate, but something as simple as receiving letters and filling out paperwork in their most comfortable language can make a significant difference in a parent's willingness to trust and engage.

Parental rights and responsibilities are not something that people are born knowing, nor are they constant across cultures. For immigrant parents, the standard for parental engagement in academics is almost certainly different in the United States than in their country of origin. Schools must take this into account, and in some cases, educating the parents is the first step to educating the child. As a child attending a K–8 elementary school in the Mexican barrios of South Chicago, my parents never questioned my teachers or principal about what they were teaching or what I was learning. For the nine years I attended that school, they firmly believed that my teachers knew best and that they should not be questioned about their methods or their discipline system. They were educated, professional, and devoted to public service. The teachers were always right because they had my best interests in mind. That was the conventional wisdom of the time, the status quo supported by the preponderance of Hispanic/Latino families of the barrio where I lived, grew up, and went to school.

Fast-forward to today, and things are beginning to change. More and more parents want to be informed. As a principal, I have been questioned countless times about any number of school initiatives. As a district administrator, I have been challenged on the decisions I have made regarding textbook selections, budget allocations, and personnel moves, to name a few. I have always welcomed parents' questions and saw them as a form of advocacy and need for clarification. I firmly believe that the questions asked by parents and families made me a better educator and more aware of the clients I was serving. One of the most important advocacy strategies that I include in my work as a trainer, consultant, parent educator, and scholar working with Hispanic/Latino parents and families, often from the most poverty-stricken and disenfranchised communities, is the use of direct, explicit, and contextually relevant essential questions.

I have identified five program areas that emphasize degrees of equity, access, and opportunity in table 1.4.

Table 1.5 (page 20) provides six facets of the whole child framework and their relevant questions for parents. Further details on utilizing the whole child framework can be found in The Whole Child in chapter 2. Teachers may want to send English and Spanish versions of these questions home to parents at the beginning of every school year so all families can begin with some concrete means of engagement.

"How will my child . . ." "Will my child have . . ." What will my child's teacher . . ."—these are stems that typically begin some of the questions using the whole child framework. Parents who are involved in the education of their children should be commended. Those who may not know how to be involved should be taught

## Table 1.4: Essential Questions: An Advocacy Tool

| | |
|---|---|
| Communication/Outreach | ‣ Are announcements reminding parents about the opportunity for education services made clearly and regularly publicized, including in other languages?<br>‣ Do school or district leaders routinely meet with and report to stakeholder groups on the status of serving Hispanic/Latino students?<br>‣ Does the district have a parent association and are meetings conducted in Spanish as well as English?<br>‣ Does the school and/or district create liaisons with community organizations and use community resources to contribute to services for Hispanic/Latino students?<br>‣ Does the school and/or district provide a training program for parents and community members? |
| Data Analysis | ‣ Is the data collected by the school and district disaggregated and analyzed and included in school and district communication?<br>‣ Does the district work with diverse stakeholder groups in interpreting education data on Hispanic/Latino students?<br>‣ Is the effectiveness of programs, products, and services on Hispanic/Latino students evaluated annually? |
| Curriculum and Instruction | ‣ Does the instructional design of education services include specific objectives on cultural diversity, cross-cultural communication, and accommodating diverse learning profiles?<br>‣ How are teachers trained to implement rigorous curriculum and instruction with Hispanic/Latino students, including those who are gifted, advanced, and high-ability?<br>‣ Do Hispanic/Latino students have opportunities for accelerated learning options? |
| Infrastructure and Policy | ‣ Does the district have a policy that advocates for its Hispanic/Latino students?<br>‣ Have academic education goals and objectives been put into place or modified as a result of data analysis?<br>‣ Does the district have the infrastructure (people, services, and finances) to support its Hispanic/Latino students? |
| Leadership | ‣ Do school and district leaders identify key personnel/experts to help make recommendations on how to best serve Hispanic/Latino students?<br>‣ Have school and district leaders received responsive, inclusively planned professional development about issues specific to Hispanic/Latino students?<br>‣ Do support services (special education, therapists, psychologists, counselors, etc.) work collaboratively on behalf of Hispanic/Latino students? |

## Table 1.5: Essential Questions Using a Whole Child Framework

| Challenged | ▸ What services provided by the school will challenge my child?<br>▸ Will my child have access to a continuum of service options to meet his/her needs that includes content and grade acceleration?<br>▸ Will my child have opportunities to question, think critically, seek solutions to problems, and reflect on his/her learning experiences? |
|---|---|
| Supported | ▸ Does the school and district support budget equity and access to federal funds to supplement their continuum of services for Hispanic/Latino students?<br>▸ What products and services support Hispanic/Latino students, particularly gifted, advanced, and high-ability students?<br>▸ If my child's achievement is not commensurate with his/her ability, what services are available to support and reverse underachievement?<br>▸ If I suspect my child has a disability, how do I access services to address his/her needs? |
| Motivated/Engaged | ▸ How will my child's teachers keep him/her engaged and motivated?<br>▸ What will my child's teachers do to increase his/her intrinsic motivation? |
| Healthy | ▸ What services will be provided for my child to address his/her social and emotional health?<br>▸ What are the education goals to ensure that my child learns about and practices living a healthy lifestyle? |
| Safe and Secure | ▸ How do the school and district ensure that services for Hispanic/Latino students receive appropriate space and equipment and take place in facilities that are safe?<br>▸ How does the teacher foster my child becoming more responsible for his/her own learning in a safe, respectful, and meaningful way? |
| Qualified | ▸ Will my child have access to highly qualified staff who are not only effective but caring and culturally competent?<br>▸ What is the school or district plan to recruit, train, and retain teachers to work with Hispanic/Latino students, particularly those identified as gifted, advanced, and high-ability? |

through partnerships with the school, district, and other community social service agencies and organizations. In those public schools receiving Title I monies, there is an expectation of parental involvement. It is part of the Title I legislation (Elementary and Secondary Education Act of 1965).

Parents should be aware of not only their responsibilities as advocates but also of their rights as patrons of the school system. To this end, a Bill of Rights for Hispanic Parents and Families (Castellano, 2016) has been adapted by the author. This publication is timely in light of then United States secretary of education Arne Duncan's announcement during the 2015 National PTA Conference about the need for a document that clearly spells out a parent's rights in advocating not only for his or her child but all children (Duncan, 2015). Hispanic parents and families have a right to:

**Table 1.6: Bill of Rights for Hispanic Parents and Families**

| | | |
|---|---|---|
| 1. | Be communicated with, verbally and in writing, in their heritage language | ▸ Websites, local radio, newspapers, social media, automated messages<br>▸ Flyers in local community businesses and faith institutions |
| 2. | Be valued and respected as an individual | ▸ Effective cross-cultural communication and understanding<br>▸ School and district leaders are culturally competent<br>▸ Awareness of intra-ethnic differences among Hispanic groups |
| 3. | Ask questions and expect answers in a timely manner and in terms that are understandable | ▸ Program goals and objectives<br>▸ Financial commitment to Hispanic/Latino students<br>▸ Educating the whole child<br>▸ Review of school and district data |
| 4. | Visit their child's classroom and school at any time | ▸ Welcoming office climate<br>▸ Parent resource center |
| 5. | Be part of decision making that impacts every aspect of their children's education | ▸ School- and district-based committees<br>▸ Policy development |
| 6. | Expect a world-class education for their children, including access to a curriculum that is rigorous and responsive to individual needs, interests, and talents | ▸ Review programs, products, and services |
| 7. | Evaluate the effectiveness and responsiveness to issues identified by Hispanic/Latino parents and families | ▸ Formally and informally<br>▸ Level of commitment to working with parents and families<br>▸ Participation in decision making |
| 8. | Expect when there are issues related to their child's academic, social, or emotional development that concerns will be taken seriously and appropriate services will be implemented in a timely manner | ▸ Opportunities for enrichment and acceleration<br>▸ Access to a continuum of services<br>▸ Financial commitment |

Continued →

| 9. Have their children receive education services in their home school and community | ‣ Question of equity and access<br>‣ Responsive to family needs |
|---|---|
| 10. Expect their child will be taught by a highly qualified teacher | ‣ Question of equity and access<br>‣ Level of infrastructure support of school and district<br>‣ Stagnant or fluid opportunities<br>‣ Training to be culturally responsive and culturally competent |

Promoting this cross-cultural communication and understanding reflects a degree of cultural competency and partnership among three very important stakeholder groups: parents, school-based personnel, and district-level leaders. When these stakeholder groups are in alignment, a collaborative, boots-on-the-ground parent and family involvement model has the potential to be very effective. As figure 1.1 shows, each plays an important role in ensuring that the academic success and potential of each child/student is the overarching priority (Castellano, 2016).

**Parents and Families to Children**

- Secure required vaccinations and physicals for school
- Reinforce the importance of attending school/daily attendance
- Communicate openly and honestly about school expectations and daily school experiences
- Ensure grade-level school supplies are available in the home
- Monitor television and technology use
- Explain importance of sleep/rest, proper nutrition, and cleanliness

| Parents and Families to Parents and Families | Parents and Families to Schools | Schools to Parents and Families | Districts to Parents and Families |
|---|---|---|---|
| ‣ Serve as mentors<br>‣ Share personal stories<br>‣ Attend meetings together<br>‣ Promote communication and understanding<br>‣ Establish community of parents<br>‣ Share knowledge<br>‣ Recruit others as volunteers in school activities<br>‣ Inspire each other to make a difference | ‣ Be on time for meetings<br>‣ Be prepared/ ask questions<br>‣ Accept answers<br>‣ Attend as a family/ extended family<br>‣ Share personal stories<br>‣ Serve as a resource to your child's school<br>‣ Advocate for services and programs<br>‣ Join a committee/be part of decision making | ‣ Use interpreters<br>‣ Plan for child care by ages<br>‣ Translate documents<br>‣ Use automated messages and social media in Spanish<br>‣ Talk with parents, not at them<br>‣ Allow opportunities for decision making<br>‣ Confirm agenda items are relevant/ contextual<br>‣ Demonstrate cultural competency | ‣ Use interpreters and greeters<br>‣ Translate documents<br>‣ Seek input and feedback<br>‣ Follow up with parent matters<br>‣ Talk with parents, not at them<br>‣ Allow opportunities for decision making<br>‣ Confirm agenda items are relevant/ contextual<br>‣ Demonstrate cultural competency |

**Figure 1.1: Boots-on-the-ground parent involvement model.**

## Parents to Students

Just as schools have an inherent responsibility to educate the students they serve, parents have an equal, if not greater, responsibility to ensure their children are prepared to be successful. Raising resilient children who are able to persevere in today's complex society is no easy task. Parents must compete with the latest technology, social media, the child's peer group, and the demands placed on them at work and at home. For those Hispanic/Latino parents also going to school, pursuing their own education, there is the additional pressure of finding time to devote to the nuclear and/or extended family. Despite the challenges that often present themselves, parents are bound to engage and interact as their child's first teacher. A child who is able to exhibit self-regulation, effort, and discipline will most likely do well in school. Teachers and other educators will attest that these skills are not only important for school but also in life. So, then, how do Hispanic/Latino parents and families instill effort and discipline in their child? This open-ended question has an infinite number of responses, often framed by a parent's own experiences as a child, but here are a few:

- Parent modeling
  - Trying difficult tasks and discussing the process with their children
  - Enrolling in an adult ESL class or other lifelong learning classes
  - Being an active participant in the student's homework while remaining calm and focused
- Extracurricular participation
  - Child enrollment in sports, art, or music clubs and teams where the student learns to be reliable
  - Parent being an active participant in home practice and preparation with a focus on *improvement* over *winning*
  - Playdates with other children (also an excellent time for parents to convene)
  - Child participating in community service projects sponsored by the school or a local agency
- Emotional availability
  - Encouraging and supporting the child's feelings
  - Listening and keeping lines of communication open—not responding in anger when the child comes to you for help
  - Sharing family meals on a regular basis

Castellano and Francis (2014) state that when primary stakeholders communicate and collaborate as a matter of routine, a school's ability to develop the talent and potential of its students increases exponentially. Within such a framework, everyone is a partner. Murphey, Guzman, and Torres (2014) document that for most Latinos, there are few things that are more important than family. Schools that understand this about Hispanic/Latino parents and families have an easier time engaging and collaborating with them. By creating an environment of trust through dialogue, schools can engage with the whole family to promote student success.

## Parents and Families to Parents and Families

Parents and families are a child's greatest advocates. Coming together to share stories, to promote communication and understanding, and to find their voice is not only empowering but also assures them that they are not alone, that there are other parents and families who share similar challenges and expectations and who ask the same questions. Parents and families working together, sharing experiences and ideas, ensures a successful pathway for their children. Parents and families who have successfully navigated the school system are in a position to mentor others and serve as a conduit of information, knowledge, inspiration, and trust. Parents and families may work together to:

+ Arrange carpooling/walking to school together as a way to support one another, build trust, and strengthen relationships

+ Meet at the local public library, community center, or school to participate in age- and/or grade-level literacy experiences

+ Exchange contact information for the purposes of sharing resources, building a support system, communicating about school issues, and serving as mentors

+ Coordinate schedules for playdates, field trips, and other such experiences

## Parents and Families to Schools

Parents and families have a responsibility to the schools their children attend. At the most basic level, they must ensure that their child is fed, is clean, has received the required vaccinations, and attends school regularly, that they do not become an attendance problem. For some parents, this is the extent of their participation. For other Hispanic/Latino parents and families, involvement in the education of their children takes on other forms. Investing time to attend school events is a beginning, as is serving as a resource to the school or joining a school-based committee. Asking questions is essential for increased understanding and clarity of expectations. With the correct information, parents become empowered to serve as advocates and become part of important decision-making bodies. Parents should strive to:

+ Visit their child's classroom and talk to their child's teacher at least once a quarter

+ Return questionnaires, surveys, applications, and such in a timely manner; keep school informed of any change of address and phone number in order to be reached immediately in case of an emergency

- Follow through on class or grade-level routines that are part of their child's educational and academic experience
- Share resources with the teachers and/or principal that would benefit others

## Schools to Parents and Families

Parents and families should expect their child to be taught by a highly qualified teacher. This is simply a nonnegotiable, particularly for those who attend Title I schools or who may be culturally, linguistically, or ethnically diverse. As such, teachers and school administrators have a responsibility to routinely inform parents on the progress of their child. They should be expected to include information on each child's academic, cognitive, and social and emotional growth and development. Teachers should become partners with parents and families, agreeing on common goals and objectives and how to maximize the talent and potential of each individual child. This approach is collaborative and child-centered. Culturally responsive schools use multimedia sources in Spanish to effectively communicate with parents, have interpreters available, arrange for child care, and affirm that meeting agenda items are relevant and contextual.

## Districts to Parents and Families

District leaders support Hispanic/Latino parents and families by acknowledging their diversity and aligning programs, products, and services to meet their unique needs—e.g., interpreters at meetings, the translation of district documents into Spanish, and opportunities for collaboration. They keep the Hispanic/Latino community informed by routinely meeting with them and reporting on the overall academic achievement of their children as a group. They seek input and feedback from parents and families and allow opportunities to engage in decision-making processes. Trust, respect, and a commitment to team work allow district leaders to build a partnership that is both supportive of, and dependent on, open and transparent communication with parents and families. Districts with this degree of accountability maximize equity, access, and opportunities for students, parents, and families.

# Conclusion

Using schools to promote hope, inspiration, and efficacy is fundamental to changing the status quo for all students, parents, and families. For Hispanic/Latino parents, families, and communities, this level and quality of engagement is foundational to promoting a culture of influence in the form of advocacy, participation, and shared decision making. The unique needs of unaccompanied minors who emigrate to the United States, the toxic stress of untreated trauma, the educational gaps Hispanic/Latino students experience, and the limited role of government in addressing these issues make parental involvement critical for the success of Hispanic/Latino students. On the politically neutral ground of schools, all families can find their chance for success. As this chapter has demonstrated, this is especially true for students who are undocumented immigrants or who are the children of immigrants. After risking everything to leave their home country and begin again in the United States, these immigrant families face discrimination and open hostility. Today more than ever, our students are tuned in to the news, social media, and the opinions of their peers. When we have a culture that makes the building of a border wall and increased hiring of immigration and customs enforcement officers a priority over more funding for education and inclusiveness, that sends a message. By acting as pillars of the community and building bridges between stakeholders, schools can be one of the single most positive influences on a child's life.

It is imperative that school and district leaders understand and embrace the intra-ethnic diversity that they may find among the Hispanic/Latino parents and families they serve. This does not mean that any identified goal, policy, or agenda item must change, but rather that how the information is delivered may have to change. Local relevancy and context will determine what that will look like. The boots-on-the-ground collaborative parent and family engagement model serves as a reference point for school and district leaders to consider. Fundamentally, the vast majority of Hispanic/Latino parents and families understand the value of education and the positive impact it has on one's life and future. They want their children to succeed. Many sacrifice to give their children that opportunity. Those who are actively involved in the education of their children stand a better chance in actualizing this hope. Those who are not actively involved may simply not know how to be. In these instances, the school and district have a responsibility to show them, and that starts with realizing why this change is so necessary. Parents, school personnel, and district leaders—all the stakeholder groups—are variables in a success equation when it comes to the education of children.

# CHAPTER 2

# The Role of Poverty

Poverty had been a way of life as far back as he could remember. Actually, he didn't even know he was poor because it seemed everyone else in the barrio lived the same way—day-by-day, week-by-week. There were seven people in his family who shared a three-bedroom, rat- and roach-infested bottom flat of a three-story building. He hated opening up a cupboard for fear of what he might find or what would jump out. His three sisters shared the largest of the three bedrooms, his parents the next largest, and he and his brother shared a bed in the smallest bedroom. They had one bathroom with a tub. They constantly used the plunger. It was an old building with even older plumbing. They all argued for bathroom time. Often, breakfast, lunch, and dinner consisted of rice, beans, and homemade tortillas. On occasion, a Spam or bologna sandwich broke up the monotony.

" He doesn't remember ever getting new clothes or shoes, but he got secondhand clothing from Angel's, a version of Goodwill in that barrio of that time. His entire family were victims of abuse at the hands of his father. His mother often took the worst of the beatings. His early, and often daily, exposure to abuse, neglect, and violence in the home and in the neighborhood made him street wise and a smart-ass, both in the classroom and in the barrio. He, along with his siblings, spent countless hours in the streets. What was there to go home to? His mother was a laborer in the factories, and his father, when working, had a job in the steel mills. They had little time for the children. He remembers having to call in sick for his mother who couldn't go to work because of her black eyes or battered body and for his father because he was passed out drunk, preferring to spend his money on other women and booze instead of spending time with his wife and children or buying groceries.

He was not especially close to his siblings growing up. They did all they could to survive childhood. They all had their separate lives and personal demons to contend with. Despite the many hardships of poverty, he did

Continued →

exceptionally well in school, which came easy for him. He was one of the lucky ones. School turned out to be a refuge, a sanctuary where he could forget.

In high school, he received free lunch and was provided a bus pass so that he did not have to walk to school. What school personnel didn't know was that waiting for the bus in a different neighborhood was as dangerous as walking. He walked, having to watch his back constantly.

There was so much about him that the school did not know.

What is the promise of America? Is it marriage, two children, a dog, and a home with a white picket fence? Is it a job that provides health and dental insurance? Is it owning a home and a car? Is it receiving an education that identifies strengths, talents, and potential? Is it all of the above? For many of our Hispanic/Latino students, the promise of America seems on a distant horizon. One of the primary causes of this distance is poverty. The evidence is in the data. In February of 2013, the US Census Bureau issued an American Community Survey Brief on the poverty rates for selected Hispanic groups by state and place that spanned the years 2007–2011. As defined by the United States Census Bureau (2013), the American Community Survey (ACS) is a nationwide survey designed to provide communities with reliable and timely demographic, social, economic, and housing data for the nation, states, congressional districts, counties, and other localities. According to the report, in 2013 the Hispanic population had an overall poverty rate of 23.2 percent, about 9 percentage points higher than the overall US rate. Among Hispanics by country of origin, national poverty rates included the following:

- Spaniard     14%
- Colombian     16%
- Cuban     16.2%
- Ecuadorian     18%
- Salvadoran     18.9%
- Guatemalan     24.9%
- Mexican     24.9%
- Puerto Rican     25.6%
- Dominican     26.3%
- Honduran     28%

The Annie E. Casey Foundation is a private philanthropy that creates a brighter future for the nation's children by developing solutions to strengthen families, build paths to economic opportunity, and transform struggling communities into safer and healthier places to live, work, and grow. In its 2016 *KIDS COUNT Data Book*, the Annie E. Casey Foundation reports that in the domain of economic well-being:

- Children living in poverty worsened from 18 percent in 2008 to 22 percent in 2014, for a total of 15,686,000 children living in poverty. For Hispanic children, the poverty rate in 2014 was 32 percent.

- Children whose parents lack secure employment also worsened during this period, from 27 percent in 2008 to 30 percent in 2014, for a total of 22,061,000 children. For Hispanic children, the rate in 2014 was 35 percent.

- Children living in households with a high housing cost improved from 39 percent in 2008 to 35 percent in 2014, totaling 25,710,000 children. For Hispanic children, the rate in 2014 was 46 percent.

- Teens not in school and not working also improved from 8 percent in 2008 to 7 percent in 2014, totaling 1,255,000 teens. For Hispanic children, the rate in 2014 was 9 percent.

The vast majority of Hispanic/Latino students attending our nation's public schools are poor. The purpose of this chapter is to help teachers, administrators, parents, and all other advocacy groups better understand and communicate with one another about the intersection between Hispanic/Latino students, their education, and the impact of poverty and to identify and apply research and practice that are responsive to their unique needs. We'll examine the impact of poverty through unstable homes, limited resources for the neediest students, and early childhood intervention. Accounting for a student's physical, mental, and emotional well-being is critical to his or her education; this is especially true for students living in poverty. Techniques for comprehensive support will be examined through the whole child framework.

## An Unstable Home

Poverty is a disruptive force. It compounds every other issue Hispanic/Latino students face at every point in their education. Poverty is such a pervasive force it is impossible to name every ramification—imagine all the consequences of poverty you can and then understand there are a hundred more. An unstable home environment may seem like an obvious aspect of a very low-income life, but the facets of instability are innumerable. This section will explore some of poverty's effects on the home's ability to prepare a child for school, from prenatal to preK.

Before a child is born he or she is already being influenced by his or her environment. Low-income mothers are less likely to receive the medical care and prenatal support their children need than their wealthier peers. Pregnant mothers may have to continue working up to the birth of the child and return to work shortly afterward. The stress and often labor-intensive tasks of low-paying jobs, as well as poor nutrition and lack of medical support, have very real effects on the baby. According to ZERO to THREE (2017), nearly 50 percent of America's babies live in or near poverty. The group adds that this is a clear warning sign for America's global competitiveness; almost half of our future workforce is already in jeopardy of falling behind from the very start.

Hispanic/Latino children raised in poverty are not loved less by their parents than wealthier children. Poverty does not equal neglect. What poverty *does* mean is that in the hierarchy of needs, poor families are often caught on the basic levels. The need for food, shelter, and security is far more pressing than the need for emotional and educational support. According to the Annie E. Casey Foundation (2014), 42 percent of Hispanic/Latino children lived in single-parent families. The Foundation further reports that children growing up in single-parent families typically have access to fewer economic and emotional resources than children in two-parent families. When we take an explicit look at the education of the adults of a Hispanic/Latino household, we find that only 11 percent of this ethnic group have a mother with at least a bachelor's degree. Furthermore, only 63 percent of Hispanic/Latino children live in a home with a parent with at least a high school diploma. Children raised in poverty are less likely to be read to, less likely to have someone practice vocabulary and numbers with them, and less likely to have educational resources in the home, such as age-accessible books and counting games. Hispanic/Latino children raised in poverty, or any child who comes from a low-income family, are not less intelligent than their peers; they have fewer means of cultivating that intelligence.

Environmental factors, not genetic deficits, explain IQ differences among poor minorities. "How many books are in the home and how good the teacher is may be questions to consider for a middle-class child, but those questions are much more important when we are talking about children raised in poverty," claims Turkheimer, a psychologist at the University of Virginia, and his colleagues Haley, D'Onofrio, Waldron, and Gottesman (2003). Turkheimer's work is part of a new wave of research that embraces a more dynamic view of the relationship between genes, heritability, and environment. Specifically, his research states that the heritability of IQ at the low end of the wealth spectrum was just 0.10 on a scale of 0 to 1, while it was 0.72 for families of high socioeconomic status. Conversely, the importance of environmental influences on IQ was four times stronger in the poorest families than in the higher-status families. The thinking is that minorities and the poor (two categories with so much overlap that researchers find it difficult to tease out their effects) perform worse not because of their genes but because they are raised in an environment lacking in resources (Turkheimer et al., 2003).

The Annie E. Casey Foundation (2016) reports that despite their high levels of economic need, Hispanics, particularly those in immigrant families, have lower rates of participation in many government support programs when compared to other racial/ethnic minority groups. This is when schools as pillars of the community can have a significant impact. Though it is difficult to identify the students in need of extra support before they are enrolled in class, if the school is a safe space for families, parents may be more willing to reach out for assistance during the critical learning time that comes with pre-enrollment. Posting notices of available resources around the school lets parents pass on the information by word of mouth, and teacher announcements to students and home letters can help younger siblings receive enrichment materials. Here are three low-cost ways to provide enrichment materials for a more stable home life:

1. Assigning homework that involves younger siblings or relatives

    ‣ Reading a story together, summarizing passages, identifying main themes

    ‣ Completing a math worksheet together, half grade-level curriculum and half simple math

    ‣ Writing a story together where participants alternate sentences, with the student handwriting the story and the sibling illustrating it

    ‣ Looking for things around the apartment, house, or duplex that reinforce simple and complex geometric designs and patterns

    ‣ Talking about the feelings that different characters in a story may have; sharing personal stories of hope and inspiration and what that means

2. Including younger children/siblings in decision making

    ‣ Reviewing and agreeing to a weekly family dinner menu

    ‣ Talking about and agreeing to individual routines, chores, and responsibilities (cleaning room, making bed, completing homework, picking up toys, bedtime routine, etc.)

    ‣ Making decisions on weekend activities and visits with family and friends

    ‣ Reaching an agreement on the amount of television (what programming) or computer time (what games) per day

3. Promoting enrichment experiences through books

    ‣ Read an ebook together

    ‣ Plan an indoor picnic including foods from a specific letter (*g*: grapes, green beans, goat cheese, guacamole)

    ‣ Survey family members about their favorite book

    ‣ Read riddle books together; have children create their own riddles

## Early Childhood Intervention

Simply put, the earlier children are in school, the more they learn. This is especially true for Hispanic/Latino students, aged three and four, who have the lowest participation rate in early childhood programs in the nation (60 percent) as compared to whites, blacks, and Asians—and all subgroups, for that matter. Early education is an important part of the equation in preparing this population to be ready for and successful in kindergarten. Prekindergarten and other early childhood–based programs are the foundation for higher levels of academic achievement, cognitive growth and development, positive interpersonal relationships, and the discovery of potential. Poverty severely limits a parent's ability to enroll his or her child in early education.

Head Start is a program of the US Department of Health and Human Services that provides comprehensive early childhood education, health, nutrition, and parent involvement services to low-income children and their families. Children from three to five years of age from families with low income, according to the poverty guidelines published by the federal government, are eligible for Head Start. The program promotes school readiness, aims to help break the cycle of poverty, and provides school- and community-based enrichment experiences to promote language development, experiential learning, and hands-on activities. Supported by Lutheran Services of Florida and Hispanic Human Resources Council of Palm Beach County, the Luciano Martinez Child Development Center in West Palm Beach, Florida, serves 131 students in its Head Start programs.

Early Head Start is a federally funded community-based program for low-income families with pregnant women, infants, and toddlers up to age three. The program was designed in 1994 by the Advisory Committee on Services for Families with Infants and Toddlers formed by the secretary of health and human services at the time. Much like Head Start, health, nutrition, and parent involvement services are offered.

There are simply not enough early intervention programs with enough spots for all the children in need of their services. Hispanic/Latino prekindergartners are more likely to be babysat by a relative than enrolled in an institution because of the cost of private daycare and limited availability of government-subsidized preK. The strong family ties found in Hispanic/Latino culture means that young children in all income groups are more likely to be with a grandmother or aunty while their parents work instead of in preschool. This is not inherently a bad thing; strong family bonds are a source of stability and comfort. Given the overstretched nature of our education budgets at national, state, and local levels, it is unlikely more early intervention programs are going to be available anytime soon, and the likelihood that they will be dual lingual for English and Spanish learning is even further removed. But the overwhelming research demonstrating the positive benefits of early intervention demands to be heard, and the continual push for greater availability must come from all stakeholders.

The National Education Association (NEA) (2013) states that research shows that providing a high-quality education for children before they turn five yields significant long-term benefits. One well-known study, the HighScope Perry Preschool Study, found that individuals who were enrolled in a quality preschool program ultimately earned up to $2,000 more per month than those who were not. Young people who are in preschool programs are more likely to graduate from high school, to own homes, and to have longer marriages. Other studies, like the Abecedarian Project, show similar results. Children in quality preschool programs are less likely to repeat grades, need special education, or get into future trouble with the law.

Making the benefits of early childhood intervention clear to parents and families is absolutely necessary. If a child is not enrolled in preK, his or her guardian during the day should be providing him or her with the enrichment and building blocks that can lead to a lifetime of success. If all students began kindergarten on equal footing, teachers could spend their energy pushing forward in the curriculum, rather than playing catch-up.

## Limited Resources

Of course, enrichment comes at a price. Limited resources are an issue for every aspect of low-income students' lives; they are more likely to live in a home without learning tools, live in a community without many public services, and attend a school with budget deficits. The US Government Accountability Office (2016) confirms that the vast majority of Hispanic/Latino children live in poorer communities and attend schools where poverty and low levels of academic achievement are the norm. The connection between poverty and achievement has been well established in research and in professional literature and publications, making poverty highly correlated to, and a primary variable for, why Hispanics/Latinos do less well in school. This section examines the effects of poverty on the availability of key resources that wealthier families and school districts take for granted: social services, qualified teachers and schools, and a diverse learning community.

In 2016, the Government Accountability Office reported that students attending schools with lower average family income learned at a slower pace than students attending schools where income was higher—not because low-income students are naturally less adept but because they have so many fewer options for enrichment. In communities with a significant number of Hispanic/Latino residents living in poverty, local resources are tapped to their limits. The result for residents in need of any combination of social services is that they are denied access and opportunity, often having to wait months for an appointment. One example is Child Find, which is a requirement designed to discover whether a child has special learning needs, to identify what those needs are, and to provide the programs and services that will best address them. The problem is that while the service is available, parents often have to wait months to get their child evaluated, thus denying the child, parent, and family access to the programs and services they need.

Part of the Bill of Rights for Hispanic Parents and Families, first developed by the author in 2016, includes the right to a highly qualified teacher. Schools defined by their poverty levels, achievement levels, and location make it more difficult for the principal and human resources office to attract the best teachers. As a result, Hispanic/Latino students are being taught by teachers who are younger, more inexperienced, or teaching in an area or grade for which they have not prepared. As a former director of bilingual education for a suburban school district of Chicago, finding teachers, let alone Spanish-speaking teachers, who had experience working with low-income and non-English or limited English-speaking Hispanic/Latino students was always a struggle despite incentives such as signing bonuses, professional development opportunities, or free tuition stipends to pursue additional teaching certificates and endorsements. Often, students would go days or weeks without a teacher with the proper certification or credentials. When teachers were eventually found, often by word of mouth, everyone in the school and district breathed a collective sigh of relief.

The US Government Accountability Office, the Office for Civil Rights, and the US Department of Education acknowledge that when compared to their white and Asian counterparts, Hispanic/Latino students attend school in older buildings with poorer facilities and limited resources. These Title I schools are often recognized for having access to fewer materials and supplies, as well as limited programs and services, thus exacerbating the debate on equity, access, and opportunity. Enrollment in math courses such as Algebra, Algebra II, Geometry, and Calculus may increase a student's access to a higher education. However, there is a stark difference in these course offerings between low-poverty and high-poverty schools. The US Government Accountability Office (2016) also reports that during the 2011–2012 school year, 79 percent of low-poverty schools offered Algebra, while 49 percent of high-poverty schools did so. During this same period, 88 percent of low-poverty schools offered Algebra II, while 75 percent of high-poverty schools did so. In Geometry, the difference was 92 to 86 percent, and the greatest difference between low-poverty and high-poverty schools is in the offering of Calculus, 71 to 29 percent.

Boschma and Brownstein (2016) state that in the one hundred largest cities in the United States, students of color are much more likely to attend schools where most of their peers are poor or low-income. This systemic economic and racial isolation looms as a huge obstacle for efforts to make a quality education available to all students. Researchers have found that the single most powerful predictor of racial gaps in education achievement is the extent to which students attend schools surrounded by other low-income students.

The Government Accountability Office (2016) was asked to examine poverty and race in schools and the progress made by the Departments of Education and Justice, which are responsible for enforcing federal civil rights laws prohibiting racial discrimination against students. From school years 2000–2001 to 2013–2014 (the most recent data available), the percentage of all K–12 public schools that had high percentages of poor black and Hispanic/Latino students grew from 9 to 16 percent. As per the Government Accountability Office's (2016) documentation, these schools were the most racially and economically concentrated: 75 to 100 percent of the students were black or Hispanic/Latino and eligible for free or reduced-price lunch—a commonly used indicator of poverty. They further add that an analysis of education data also found that compared with other schools, these schools offered disproportionately fewer math, science, and college preparatory courses and had disproportionately higher rates of students who were held back in ninth grade, suspended, or expelled. All in all, 48 percent of Hispanic/Latino students attend high-poverty schools.

When low-income, racially, culturally, and linguistically diverse students attend school with others just like them school improvements efforts are confounded. Consequently, the impact on the nation's workforce may be negatively affected. During his interview with Boschma and Brownstein (2016), Dr. Sean F. Reardon from Stanford University states, "We can look at every poor district in the United States and see if there are any that are doing reasonably well, where Hispanic kids are performing at least at the national average. And the answer is virtually none. You can find isolated schools that are doing better than you would predict. But the weight of socioeconomic disadvantage is really quite big. We don't have much evidence of places that have been systemically successful when they serve large populations of low-income students. It's a big lift."

Students living in poverty or low-income areas are too often defined by what they are missing—not enough social services, not enough teachers, not enough diversity. It is too easy for us to group these struggling students into schools with financial troubles and judge their performance on standardized tests as an obvious result. More than once I have heard teachers justify the achievement gap between Title I schools and schools in wealthier districts as "Low-income kids are just bad students." This is emphatically untrue. Students from low-income families need more support from their school districts than wealthier peers to achieve the most success, and yet we respond by sequestering these students into resource deserts. Rather than a reflection on their ability to succeed, their poor performance is a reflection on our ability to set them up for failure.

## The Nation, the State, the District

Education policy is enacted and enforced at three different levels: federal, state, and local. The idea is that national policy standards can be set by the federal government, while states have the authority to design policy implementation, and local districts can customize their approach to specific student populations. Districts inform states of their student needs, states allocate resources based on this personalized approach, and the federal government provides subsidies and reimbursements for states to further invest in education. In this way, there are three levels of protection for students and families, and education is tailored to the widely varying needs of our more than 50 million public school students. It is a student-centric model of policy creation. In reality, we know this is not the case. The three levels of authority have become bureaucratic nightmares with sometimes conflicting and almost always reactionary policy. Poverty further complicates this picture—the allocation of money and resources is not distributed based on student need but on innumerable other factors including test scores. This section will examine how poverty complicates the role of the federal level through miscounting of students, the state level through misappropriation of funds, and the district level through achievement gaps.

## The Nation

The Child Trends Hispanic Institute (2016) reports that over the next few years, critical decisions will be made on how the 2020 US Census will be conducted, revealing certain issues associated with the undercount of young Hispanic/Latino children, while providing recommendations to improve the accuracy of the count in the next census. A more accurate count would make the allocation of resources to these children and families more equitable and in line with their actual numbers. Currently, more than 24 percent of US children under age five are Hispanic, and this proportion is projected to grow to 32 percent by 2050. Nearly two-thirds (62 percent) of Hispanic children live in low-income households—that is, with incomes below two times the federal poverty line. As the country's fastest-growing sector of the child population, Hispanic/Latino children's healthy development is critical to the future social and economic well-being of the country. We must wait ten years between each census to try to record the official population of these needy students. Key findings include:

> Young children have a higher net undercount rate than any other age group. Latino children account for a disproportionate share (more than 36 percent) of the total net undercount for all.

> There was a net undercount of 400,000 young Latino children ages zero to four in the 2010 census.

> Much of this undercount is concentrated in a few states, with California, Texas, Florida, Arizona, and New York accounting for almost three-quarters (72 percent) of the net undercount.

> Existing research suggests that young Latino children are undercounted because: (1) Latinos are more likely than non-Latinos to live in hard-to-count places like multiunit buildings with a higher percentage of renters; (2) Latinos are more likely than non-Latinos to live in hard-to-count families

and households, such as multigenerational and highly mobile families and households and complex relationships; and
(3) there is some evidence that Latino adults are more likely
to believe that young children do not need to be reported
on the census form.

Schools and teachers can use the following strategies to encourage accurate completion and return of census data and information:

- During math lessons on data, immerse students in census data and then encourage them to collect data at home, at school, or in their community.

- During social studies, help students understand the importance of maps and how they are used for different purposes. Teach them how to read different kinds of maps and how they can make their own (home, school, community).

- Use students as ambassadors by giving them age- and grade-appropriate information about the census and having them share it with their parents and families.

- Help students understand the importance of the census; that it is, in fact, about them, their families, and the communities in which they live; and that government resources are given to the communities with the most accurate census count. Encourage them to share the information with their parents and families.

The potential impact on states and local communities with young undercounted Hispanic/Latino children translates to fewer federal dollars, resources, programs, and services. We must have an accurate count of our student populations to prevent these children from slipping through the cracks of our education system.

## The State

The Network for Public Education (2016) believes that sustaining a public education system of high quality is a job for the entire community, whether or not they have children in public schools and even if they have no children. An investment in the community's children is an investment in the future, a duty we all share. In their *A 50 State Report Card*, they evaluate how well each of the fifty states and the District of Columbia support their public schools, based on objective and measurable factors aligned to their values. For the purpose of this chapter, the ten states with the largest Hispanic/Latino student population, according to World Atlas (2016), are:

1. New Mexico: 47%
2. California: 38%
3. Texas: 38%
4. Arizona: 30%
5. Nevada: 27%

6. Florida: 23%
7. Colorado: 21%
8. New York: 18%
9. New Jersey: 18%
10. Illinois: 16%

Table 2.1 includes these ten states along with the grades given to them by the Network for Public Education in four areas: professionalization of teaching, school finance, whether the state spends taxpayer resources wisely, and the chance for student success.

**Table 2.1: State Grades in Key Areas**

| | States with the Largest Number of Hispanic Students World Atlas (2016) | Professional Teaching | School Finance | Spend Taxpayer Resources Wisely | Chance for Success |
|---|---|---|---|---|---|
| 1 | New Mexico: 47% | D | D | D | D |
| 2 | California: 38% | C | D | C | F |
| 3 | Texas: 38% | F | D | D | F |
| 4 | Arizona: 30% | F | F | D | D |
| 5 | Nevada: 27% | C | F | F | D |
| 6 | Florida: 23% | F | D | C | D |
| 7 | Colorado: 21% | F | D | D | C |
| 8 | New York: 18% | B | B | C | D |
| 9 | New Jersey: 18% | D | D | D | D |
| 10 | Illinois: 16% | C | D | C | D |

*Source: Network for Public Education, 2016.*

This section focuses on the areas of school finance and tax spending.

*School Finance*

The Network for Public Education (2016) maintains that in order for all students to have equitable education opportunities, states must adequately and fairly fund their schools. We know that the level of poverty in a school is the single best predictor of average student performance. Money matters in education. Resources like smaller class sizes and more support staff lead to significantly higher achievement and graduation rates—especially for poor and minority students. Yet despite concerns about gaps in student performance, states have not implemented policies that address inequitable funding between schools attended by the children of the rich and the poor. The Network for Public Education (2016) further reports that during the past decade, in fact, the gap in spending between the wealthy and the poor districts grew by 44 percent. Title I is intended to offer schools with significant numbers of low-income students additional funds in an effort to balance the playing field. However, most superintendents and principals would argue this is still not enough. Inequities in school finance will continue to harm the students who need the most assistance until their chance for success becomes an equal policy priority to a higher-income student.

### Spending Taxpayer Resources Wisely

The Network for Public Education (2016) further maintains that although the amount and distribution of state funding for education is critical, how these dollars are spent is equally important. Tax dollars must be spent to reduce class size and invest in early childhood education. Because the relationship between students and teacher is vital, the Network is also concerned about the growth in online learning and virtual schools. Lower class size has been linked to improved learning and a host of other benefits, especially for students of color, students in poverty, students with disabilities, and students who are linguistically or culturally different. For a myriad of reasons, students who are not successful in traditional brick and mortar schools are being encouraged to consider online learning using virtual school formats. A virtual, computer-based education, therefore, calls for a different type of learning community. Technology may help our students prepare for the future, and increased use of computers and tablets in the classroom continues to be the strongest trend in modern education, but we must be careful that we are truly putting the student first. Diverting money to technology takes away from lowering class size and providing access to early childhood education such as full-day kindergarten or preschool programs. Are states encouraging low-income districts to enroll their students online because that is the best strategy or because that is the easiest strategy? Schools in more prosperous districts have been able to successfully combine technology and traditional schooling so students have access to advanced classes while remaining participants in a community of learners. Current reforms instead emphasize the expansion of technology.

As the chief administrator of an elementary dual-language immersion (Spanish/English) charter school in Pennsylvania, I had Hispanic/Latino students who were gifted, advanced, and high-ability in math but no teacher certified to teach advanced math courses like Algebra I. As a result, I contracted with a noted and respected publisher who provided access to a live, online math teacher for lessons, enrichment, and assessments. The school's elementary math resource teacher supervised the class during their daily math hour. Not only did the students have access to a certified Algebra I teacher, but they also had the luxury of remaining in the school with their friends and other classmates. The parents of participating students also appreciated our efforts in accommodating the advanced math ability of their children.

I would argue for a balance of online classes and community classes for schools with students of every income level, with the needs of all students serving as the overarching priority.

## The District

According to Sparks (2016), racial achievement gaps exist in nearly every community across the country with a measurable Hispanic population, and many districts with a traditional commitment to education and resources to serve all students instead have the worst inequities, according to new research comparing achievement gaps across state lines. As cited in Sparks (2016), using a database of five years of test scores from more than 40 million students nationwide, Stanford University researchers Sean Reardon, Demetra Kalogrides, and Kenneth Shores analyzed how racial achievement gaps look in different parts of the country and how segregated schools widen those gaps. Along with education professor Andrew Ho from Harvard University, they linked scale scores for state tests to the scales for the NAEP in the same grades and subjects and used that yardstick to compare average achievement gap trends for students in third through eighth grades in more than 12,000 districts across the country, from 2009 to 2013. Table 2.2 provides estimated white-Hispanic achievement gaps in twenty school districts with the largest and smallest gaps, 2009 to 2013.

Table 2.2: Twenty School Districts with the Largest and Smallest White-Hispanic Achievement Gap, 2009–2013

| | Smallest White-Hispanic Achievement Gap | | Largest White-Hispanic Achievement Gap |
|---|---|---|---|
| 1 | Detroit City School District: MI | 1 | Homewood City: AL |
| 2 | Cicero SD 99: IL | 2 | Menlo Park City Elementary: CA |
| 3 | Decatur SD 61: IL | 3 | Atlanta Public Schools: GA |
| 4 | North Syracuse Central SD: NY | 4 | Union Free SD of the Tarrytowns: NY |
| 5 | Delphi Unified: CA | 5 | Chapel-Hill-Carrboro Schools: NC |
| 6 | Socorro ISD: TX | 6 | San Rafael City Elementary: CA |
| 7 | Paramount Unified: CA | 7 | Evanston-Skokie School District 65: IL |
| 8 | Turner-Kansas City: KS | 8 | Mountain View Whisman: CA |
| 9 | Standard Elementary: CA | 9 | Berkeley Unified: CA |
| 10 | Fairfax Elementary: CA | 10 | MSD Washington Township: IN |
| 11 | Mabank ISD: TX | 11 | Cabrillo Unified: CA |
| 12 | DeSoto ISD: TX | 12 | Park City District: UT |
| 13 | Gloucester Co. Public Schools: VA | 13 | District of Columbia Public Schools |
| 14 | Marshall Co. School District: MS | 14 | Barrington CUSD 220: IL |
| 15 | Channelview ISD: TX | 15 | Summit SD North Region 1: CO |
| 16 | Hillside Township: NJ | 16 | Geneva City SD: NY |

| 17 | Ecorse Public School District: MI | 17 | Palatine CCSD 15: IL |
|----|-----------------------------------|----|----------------------|
| 18 | Sheldon ISD: TX | 18 | North Shore SD 132: IL |
| 19 | Kewanee CUSD: IL | 19 | Richfield Public SD: MN |
| 20 | Mayfield Independent: KY | 20 | Dekalb County: GA |

Several of the districts with the lowest achievement gaps have similar profiles of high poverty and multiple attempts at education overhauls, suggesting that their low achievement gaps come from lower performance overall. The wealthier school districts have bigger achievement gaps than poorer places, all else being equal, which is quite striking and disturbing since you'd hope that those places that have the most resources would be the most effective at reducing the gaps (Sparks, 2016). It is these inequities that districts should be proactive about and responsive to, both in their own policies and in their advocating at a state level. Districts are not tailoring their resources to their populations. The research of Sparks (2016) is further supported by the United States Department of Education's Office for Civil Rights (2016), which documents that when competition increases, Hispanic/Latino families often lose out. Research by the Child Trends Hispanic Institute (2017) and Child Trends Data Bank (2016) clearly shows that like black families, on average, Hispanic/Latino families live in a poor neighborhood and their children attend schools with fewer resources than white families at the same income level. Higher-income families are investing more in personal wealth in the education of their children, beyond what comes from the school. If you give a low-income student the exact same resources as an upper-income student and the need is greater for the low-income student, the gap is going to expand.

Poverty discourages equity, access, and opportunity at all three levels of policymaking. At the federal, state, and district levels, it results in miscounting, misappropriation, and missed opportunities for student success. We need to change our approach to policymaking from money-focused to student-focused. Money will always make things complicated—taxpayers want to know their contributions are being used effectively, and legislatures are always looking to reduce wasteful spending. From one perspective, public schools serve to hemorrhage money. But schools do not exist to make money as institutions. They exist because the United States recognizes education as a fundamental right for all children and as the single greatest investment we can make for our future economically. More education for more children means more adults with more money to buy more things, create more ideas, and invest in new opportunities. It starts with putting the child first.

## The Whole Child

Student-centric education means addressing the needs of the whole child. Over the past ten to fifteen years, there has been a national movement led by various education-based associations and groups, such as ASCD, state-level organizations, nonprofit special interest groups, and a plethora of schools and school districts to move beyond traditional paradigms of how public school students in the United States are educated. Looking beyond a singular focus on academic metrics, these individuals and groups understand the added importance of addressing the social and emotional needs of students. The basic premise is that if students are socially and emotionally healthy and safe, supported, engaged, and challenged, then the likelihood of successfully meeting grade-level academic standards is heightened. The highly concentrated levels of poverty typically associated with Hispanic/Latino students and the public schools located within these zones make this movement all the more critical to their chance for success. With this in mind, educating the whole child promotes a continuum of personalized services that is the heart of the movement. This section explores how schools can account for their students physically, mentally, and emotionally instead of only academically.

### Physically

Part of the whole child movement is helping students, parents, and families understand the benefits of practicing a healthy lifestyle. Lessons are taught, communications are sent home in English and Spanish, and resources are provided on a range of topics. Poverty is linked with a whole suite of negative health effects, from poor nutrition to exposure to toxic chemicals. Students from low-income and new immigrant families simply do not have access to the same health information and resources that other families do without school intervention. Two of the most significant areas in which schools can have a positive impact on student health are nutrition and sexual health.

Of all subgroups, Hispanics/Latinos have the highest prevalence of obesity. Schools can play an important role in helping to reduce the rate of obesity of Hispanic/Latino boys and girls by including responsible cafeteria meals, lessons on proper nutrition, and physical exercise. Within a school, the cafeteria menu is a logical place to start. Offering a menu of nutritious, healthy choices for breakfast and lunch is only the beginning. Schools need to explain the reasoning for their choices to students, so students can make those choices for themselves at home. The goal is to normalize certain dietary habits and ostracize others, even if those bad habits are witnessed at home. Sending home information to parents can help with this. Below are some easy, cost-effective measures that can have a huge impact:

- Posters, bulletin boards, and other media that explain portion sizes, the clinically proven dangers of excessive sugar intake, and how to read a nutrition label hung up in classrooms and the cafeteria

- A Spanish and English version of the USDA-approved "MyPlate" sent home at the beginning of the year with instructions to post it on the fridge

- Informing parents of free online resources like the USDA monthly food plans and MyPlate tip sheets, available at www.cnpp.usda.gov

- Homework assignments that include students grocery shopping with their parents and completing scavenger-hunt activities for good nutrition

- Virtual health-based field trips, visits to a farm or farmers market, or even the supermarkets

The goal is to help provide these families with the means to help themselves, through education. Further, whether through a structured physical education program, in-class experiences, or recess, schools need to encourage movement. Schools, parents, and families may use the following low-cost ways to promote physical activity with their students:

- Encourage aerobic games during free time.

  - Jumping rope can be done inside or outside.

  - Running games engage students in cardiovascular activities.

- Involve dance as a form of exercise.

  - Set apart five minutes of class to have the students get up and dance.

  - Make a playlist of your students' favorite songs (school-appropriate versions, of course) and have them design a dance to match (or learn the dance the song teaches).

- Utilize the home.

  - Have students (with a parent or older sibling) chart a one-mile path around their neighborhood for walks.

  - Make exercise part of homework; in between sets of problems, have students walk up and down their stairs five times or do five push-ups.

The Annie E. Casey Foundation (2016) documents that children's health is the foundation of their overall development, and ensuring that they are born healthy is the first step toward increasing the life chances of disadvantaged children. Poverty, poor nutrition, lack of preventive health care, substance abuse, maternal depression, and family violence put children's health at risk. Poor health in childhood impacts other critical aspects of a child's life, such as school readiness and attendance, and can have lasting consequences on his or her future health and well-being. The foundation's 2016 state-to-state comparison focused on four health indicators: low birth weight in babies, children without health insurance, child and teen deaths per 100,000, and teens who abuse alcohol or drugs. Table 2.3 identifies the ten states that have the most and least healthy children based on these criteria.

**Table 2.3: Most and Least Healthy States**

| | Most Healthy States for Children | | Least Healthy States for Children |
|---|---|---|---|
| 1 | Minnesota | 50 | Louisiana |
| 2 | Connecticut | 49 | Mississippi |
| 3 | Iowa | 48 | Wyoming |
| 4 | Massachusetts | 47 | Florida (Large Hispanic Population) |
| 5 | Washington | 46 | Arkansas |
| 6 | Rhode Island | 45 | Arizona (Large Hispanic Population) |
| 7 | New York (Large Hispanic Population) | 44 | New Mexico (Large Hispanic Population) |
| 8 | Hawaii | 43 | Colorado (Large Hispanic Population) |
| 9 | Illinois (Large Hispanic Population) | 42 | Alabama |
| 10 | Vermont | 41 | West Virginia |

The National Research Center on Hispanic Children and Families (2016) reports that Hispanic/Latino teens are also most likely to abuse alcohol or drugs (6 percent) compared to whites (5 percent) and blacks (4 percent). And as been previously reported, although the likelihood of being uninsured has declined for all racial groups, Hispanic/Latino children (10 percent) were far more likely to be uninsured than their Asian and Pacific Islander (6 percent), African American (5 percent), multiracial (5 percent), and white (5 percent) peers. Schools can play a pivotal role in helping make children healthy by focusing on preventive health care like proper nutrition.

They also report that along with whites (7.0 percent), Hispanics/Latinos (7.1 percent) have the "lowest" low birth weights compared to African American babies (12.8 percent). This may be a bit surprising as Hispanic/Latino females have the largest number of teen births (38) per 1,000 among all racial and ethnic groups. In addition, the Child Trends Hispanic Institute (2014) adds that sexually active teen Latinas (females) are less than half as likely as white females to report current use of birth control pills (11 percent and 24 percent, respectively). This disparity may contribute to why Latina teens are twice as likely as white teens to become pregnant—though in recent years they have experienced the greatest decline in pregnancy rates of all racial/ethnic groups. Schools can encourage this trend to continue. Thirty percent of all teenage girls who drop out of school cite pregnancy and parenthood as key reasons. Rates among Hispanic girls (36 percent) are higher.

These students may not receive any reproductive education from their families. If what they have to rely on is pop culture or their trusted teachers, then we must empower teachers to be the information source they turn to first. The Child Trends Hispanic Institute (2014) reports that children of teen mothers perform worse on many measures of school readiness, are 50 percent more likely to repeat a grade, and are more likely than children born to older mothers to drop out of high school.

The issue of sexual education in schools is difficult to tackle because it is an uncomfortable topic and parents do not want to consider that portion of their children's lives. While parent complaints over sex ed have dropped off in recent years, there is still controversy over how and when classes are taught. In whatever way a school may address this problem, what we have seen is that abstinence-only education does not work. The United States has one of the highest teen birth rates of any industrialized nation. Students are going to have questions, and "just say no" does not explain to them the dangers of sexually transmitted diseases (STDs) or the risks of pregnancy. It also limits the dialogue for lesbian, gay, bisexual, and transgender (LGBT) students who have no one in their family supporting their sexuality and need more than a brick wall to talk to. Schools need to coordinate with their staff to determine which books are available in the school library or which websites that can be safely accessed from school computers (without resulting in a code infraction) they can refer students to.

This book recommends MyHealthEd's Real Talk. Real Talk (https://realtalkapp.com) is a mobile app that uses real stories by real teens to convey relevant and credible information about the issues that teens go through growing up. Stories cover topics including healthy relationships, sexuality, bullying, and online safety.

## Mentally

The use of formative assessments continuously allows students the opportunity to discuss and explain and to refine their work. When student voices are activated, they express themselves freely. When teachers create "liberated zones" in their classrooms, students know they will not be judged, ridiculed, bullied, or disrespected. At the core of student engagement is the use of differentiated and open-ended, inquiry-based learning opportunities that are culturally responsive, relevant, and personalized; students demonstrate what they know and can do through both traditional means and other self-selected performance-based experiences (project-based or problem-based).

In the whole child framework, teachers and administrators are facilitators and resource providers. Rubrics generally inform the progress of students as they reflect and engage in processes of self-assessment. How they view their own work is further supported by their teachers, who provide feedback that is explicit and connected to a rubric, set of benchmarks, or performance standards. The immediate objective is to help students grow and make progress with their learning and achievement. When learning is meaningful, students give value to the teacher-learner process. They engage, they think critically, and they problem solve—hallmarks of advanced academic and cognitive growth. Student engagement is further heightened when their interests are considered, when their preferred learning styles are honored, and when there is flexibility in time management. Not all students master content at the same time or in the same way.

Ideally, all students are challenged by their teachers throughout the grade-level curriculum. Classrooms where students feel safe, nurtured, and encouraged are best suited to implement challenging learning experiences.

## Emotionally

There are several reasons why the socioemotional development of Hispanic/Latino students needs to be intentional, purposeful, and proactively nurtured. The most critical reason is that cognitive development and social and emotional development are inseparable. Findings from brain research tell us: (1) emotion has an impact on the learning process, (2) social-emotional functions can facilitate or impede cognitive processes, and (3) we remember what we have learned better and longer when emotion is a part of our learning process (Clark, 2013).

The Child Trends Hispanic Institute (2014) reports that when it comes to mental health, the data for Hispanic children and youth offer some good and some not-so-good news. More than a third of Hispanic high school students report feeling persistently sad or hopeless—a higher proportion than among white or black students, although this rate is 10 percent lower than it was in 1999. Hispanic females are particularly likely to report these feelings—nearly half in 2013. When asked to report on children's adverse family experiences—a list of events that are associated with an increased likelihood of physical and mental health problems—51 percent of Hispanic children have parents who indicated at least one such experience, compared with 44 percent of white children.

There are likely many reasons behind these emotional health disparities. The Child Trends Hispanic Institute (2014) reports that during the first few years of life, there are important opportunities for parents to meet with pediatricians, share concerns, and receive guidance on health and developmental issues. As such, well-child visits can catch problems early or prevent them. Among children ages birth through five, Hispanics/Latinos are the group least likely to have a well-child visit. A related concern is health insurance coverage. Hispanic/Latino children are covered at a rate lower than whites and blacks. And, of those Hispanic/Latino children who were born outside the United States, nearly four in ten lack health insurance. Unauthorized immigrant children have the lowest coverage of any group—only about one in five are covered. As a result of their financial hardships, and traditional Hispanic/Latino views on mental health, these children are less likely to ever receive professional counseling than their peers. One of the primary responsibilities of administrators is to ensure the safety of all adults in a school, physically and emotionally. Administrators, along with the instructional and support staff, in turn, create the same kind of climate for students as part of their commitment to educating the whole child. Essential practices include keeping the building safe, the school climate safe, and all equipment students have direct access to safe. A school culture where the race, ethnicity, and languages of the students and families are valued and respected increases the probability that students will feel empowered, motivated, and inspired to learn. Additionally, there is a shared understanding and acceptance of a code of behavioral conduct that is foundational to the concept of safety. The expectations are explicit and practiced by all groups.

An intentional focus on creating a safe and nurturing school environment is part of the whole child movement. This environment, in turn, allows Hispanic/Latino students to concentrate their efforts on learning. When a school and classroom eliminate the distraction of fear, students are more likely to do better academically. Jeff Franklin (2008), an extension educator in youth development for the University of Illinois, states that ten years of research clearly shows that social and emotional learning is foundational to children's/students' success in school, work, and life. Addressing the social and emotional needs of youth not only prepares students to learn but also increases their capacity to learn. He states that social and emotional learning (SEL) can lead to an 11 percent increase in academic performance and refers to both what we teach and how we teach. SEL involves teaching students a set of skills, a set of five core competencies, to help support their social and emotional well-being as well as a process for learning. The five core competencies that have been integrated into the Illinois Learning Standards are self-awareness, self-management, social awareness, interpersonal skills, and responsible decision-making skills.

For example, if you are upset because of an argument with a friend, you shake it off before you go to work so you can fulfill your responsibilities. Students need to learn how to have that same emotional control. Keep in mind that students who feel helpless cannot learn effectively, so it is imperative we help them develop these skills. The following activities are designed to facilitate social and emotional learning.

- Give students opportunities to share safe information about themselves and their families. One activity I use is a quick write lasting about five minutes with the prompt "If I was going to walk into your home, apartment, or condo, what would be the sights, sounds, and smells that would tell me about your culture (your racial, ethnic, cultural heritage)?" This is a very personal and empowering activity that allows students to comfortably share.

+ Challenge thinking in a safe, judgment-free zone. After students make choices based on the content they are learning or experiences they are having, ask questions relevant to the content and expect them to defend and support their choice. Once an educator has created a nurturing and trusting climate, students will be more apt to participate. For example, ask, "Why do some people recycle and others do not?"

+ Use age/grade-appropriate literature that has a lesson to be learned, a moral, or contains experiences similar to those that students in your class/ school may have. Afterward, seek feedback from students allowing them to demonstrate a complex theme such as empathy. With the undergraduate preservice teacher candidates in my university classes, I routinely read children's books to them to reinforce a particular course objective—e.g., inclusion, an appreciation for diversity, working with special needs students, and so on.

+ Allow students to select a song that inspires them, that gives them hope, or that makes them feel they can make it. I have used this strategy throughout my career as a teacher and administrator at elementary, middle, and high schools; as a professor at the undergraduate and graduate levels; and as an administrator with new and experienced teachers via professional development experiences. Feedback, across the board, is always positive, proactive, and thankful.

+ Use anchor charts, visuals, posters, and such that promote the importance of communication, collaboration, and collegiality among and between students. Model the behavioral expectations for and with students.

It is important to remember that sometimes the best teaching and leading we do is the modeling of skills and behaviors we are trying to develop in our students. They are always watching to see the behaviors and actions, or reactions, of those around them. Every day, our own use of our SEL skills can promote or create those important teachable moments (Franklin, 2008).

By accounting for all aspects of the student—physically, emotionally, and mentally instead of only academically—schools can improve the chance for success for every student, and especially low-income Hispanic/Latino students. In addition, where needed, all whole child information should be available in Spanish through both traditional (newspaper, radio, and automated phone messages) means, as well as through all social media outlets (Facebook, Snapchat, Twitter, LinkedIn, etc.) used by both state and local education agencies. The goal is to reach as wide an audience as possible. By implementing practices that allow each student to grow academically, cognitively, socially, and emotionally according to their talents and abilities, we are truly educating the whole child.

## Conclusion

Overall, Hispanic children are living at significantly higher levels of poverty than other student populations. As stated in the National Research Center on Hispanic Children and Families (2016) report titled *A National Portrait of the Health and Education of Hispanic Boys and Young Men*, Hispanic/Latino children currently make up roughly one in four of all children in the United States. Notably, 5.7 million Hispanic/Latino children, or one-third of all Hispanic/Latino children in the United States, are in poverty, more than in any other racial/ethnic group. Nearly two-thirds live in low-income families, defined as having income of less than two times the federal poverty level. By 2050, Hispanic/Latino children are projected to make up one in three of all kids in the United States, similar to that of white children. The children in our classrooms today are the parents and relatives of that next generation. This is a call to action on a nationwide, multigenerational scale; if we make a difference in the lives of today's Hispanic/Latino students, we're improving the chance of success and quality of life for students tomorrow, and next year, and thirty years from now.

Poverty makes it more difficult to achieve dreams and fulfill the promise of America. Not impossible but difficult. For Hispanic/Latino students, an education may be their best or only path for a brighter future. Our nation is filled with millions of Hispanics/Latinos who have escaped a life of poverty through hard work, a commitment to improvement, and a willingness to persevere. For the majority of them, education was the game changer. This is the message that needs to be constantly sent: education is a game changer. What we need to do now is change the game so every student is participating. As more educators adopt the whole child framework in their teaching strategies, we will see how the effects of an unstable home life, limited resources, and lack of early childhood intervention can be mitigated and overcome.

# CHAPTER 3

# The Challenge of Identity

The challenge of identity was never an issue for him as a child attending public school. He was Mexican American. That was how he was raised. It seemed just about everyone in the barrio was Mexican or Mexican American. They all went to the Spanish-speaking Catholic mass, went to Spanish-speaking stores, listened to the Spanish radio stations, and watched Spanish-language television. Most of his adult relatives spoke only Spanish. Through eighth grade, he went to school with other Mexicans and Mexican Americans. He was solid in his identity.

High school was the first time he went to school with non-Hispanics. He lived in the barrios; they lived in the hood; and they all shared poverty. Those kids spoke differently but the same. Their skin was darker, but he knew dark Mexicans, too. He was a light-skinned Mexican, probably taking after his mother, who had fair white skin, blazing red hair, and the greenest of eyes. Yes, she was Mexican, from Jalisco, Mexico. His dad was a dark Mexican.

It was the first day of high school when he began to notice he was different. And not because of his ethnicity, language, or skin color. As he entered the high school for the first time with his neighborhood friends, he turned left, and they all turned right. Left was the new building; right was the old building. Left was where the smart kids had most of their classes, and right was special education, shop class, and remedial education. He started high school as an honors student, and all of his childhood friends didn't. Yes, this was when he knew something was different.

When he entered honors English and history class, he was the only one of his kind—male, Hispanic. He felt different. The challenge of identity began to be an issue. Where were the other guys, the other Mexicans? Was this a mistake? He was too afraid to say or do anything. He let it ride. Secretly, he loved these classes. They were stimulating and challenging, and a day did not pass without learning something new, often about himself. At home, no one ever asked him about

Continued →

school or how he was doing. It didn't matter. He still loved them. His childhood friends began to change, too, calling him names for wanting to learn and for being smart. Learning came easy for him, and he was proud of that. Friendships began to slide further and further apart.

It was his junior year when he learned about GPA and class rank. He remembers some teachers being surprised that he was smart; they said it in class, in front of everyone. These were mostly the work study program teachers, and they probably singled him out because he was a smart aleck in their classes. He was in the top 10 percent of his class of 570 students, from a freshman class that began with almost 1,000 kids.

The use of the terms *Hispanic* and *Latino* to describe Americans of Spanish origin or descent is unique to the United States and their meaning continues to change and evolve. Outside the United States, these terms are not widely used and may also have different meanings. In practice, the US Census Bureau and others rely on self-reports to determine ethnicity—someone is Hispanic or Latino if they self-identify as Hispanic or Latino. Throughout the book, I have used the terms *Hispanic* and *Latino* interchangeably, depending on who is being referenced, and other times, I use them at the same time, separated by a slash. In my personal and professional lives, I have been referred to as Hispanic, Latino, Spanish, Mexican, and Mexican American. In short, *Hispanic* focuses on Spanish-speaking origin. This means Spain is included, but Brazil is not because Brazilians speak Portuguese. *Latino* refers to people of Latin American origin. This includes Brazil and excludes Spain, a European nation. Castellano (2011) reports that both terms refer to essentially the same people, but they convey different and, in some cases, opposing notions of identity.

Identity is one of the most complicated issues any young person faces. Reconciling who you are personally with who you want to be, where you come from, and how other people see you can be distressing under the best circumstances; factoring in the effects of immigration and poverty can be absolutely overwhelming. Hispanic/Latino students are not only held responsible for overcoming their own trauma and family histories of hardship but also for juggling this complicated reconciliation. Educators who are better informed on the particular difficulties their Hispanic/Latino students face in understanding who they are and their place in the world will be better able to serve this unique population.

## Demographics

The first, most crucial aspect of understanding the Hispanic/Latino identity is to realize there is no Hispanic/Latino identity—there are Hispanic/Latino people, with rich heritages and nuanced cultures, who identify with different aspects of their history and experiences. To help fight the issue of oversimplification, this section explores some of the factors Hispanic/Latino students use to inform their identity: country of origin and race.

According to the results of a 2010 Census Brief, 94 percent of Hispanic respondents (47.4 million) reported one race from the five choices presented by the United States Office of Budget Management: White, Black/African-American, American Indian or Alaska Native, Asian, or Native Hawaiian or Other Pacific Islander.

- 53.0 percent identified as White
- 36.7 percent identified as Some Other Race. Write-in codes:
  - Mexican
  - Hispanic
  - Latin American
  - Puerto Rican
  - Multiple Races
- 2.5 percent identified as Black or African American
- 1.4 percent identified as American Indian and Alaska Native
- 0.5 percent identified as Asian
- 0.1 percent identified as Native Hawaiian or Other Pacific Islander

For those Hispanics who chose Some Other Race (SOR), the top five selections were Mexican, Hispanic, Latin American, Puerto Rican, or Multiple Races. Moreover, key findings from the Pew Research Center: Hispanic Trends (2012b) include:

- When it comes to describing their identity, most Hispanics prefer their family's country of origin over pan-ethnic terms. Half (51 percent) say that most often they use their family's country of origin to describe their identity. That includes such terms as *Mexican* or *Cuban* or *Dominican*, for example. Just one-quarter (24 percent) say they use the terms *Hispanic* or *Latino* to most often describe their identity, while 21 percent say they use the term *American* most often.

- Hispanic or Latino? Most don't care, but among those who do, *Hispanic* is preferred. Half (51 percent) say they have no preference for either term. When a preference is expressed, *Hispanic* is preferred over *Latino* by more than a two-to-one margin—33 percent versus 14 percent.

- Most Hispanics do not see a shared culture among US Hispanics. Nearly seven in ten (69 percent) say Hispanics in the United States have many different cultures, while 29 percent say that Hispanics in the United States share a common culture.

These explanations may leave the reader feeling slightly dissatisfied with regards to truly identifying Hispanics/Latinos in general. If this is the case, the reader has grasped the essence of Hispanic diversity. Hispanics represent many countries of origin (see table 3.1), with the five largest groups (Mexicans, Puerto Ricans, Cubans, Dominicans, and Salvadorans) accounting for 82.2 percent of all Hispanics living in the United States. By far, the largest group of self-reporting Hispanics are those with Mexican origin, who make up 63.4 percent of all Hispanics living in the United States. The Hispanic threefold ancestry consists of contributions from peoples of Africa, Europe, and the Americas.

## Table 3.1: Hispanic or Latino Origin for the United States

| Group | Number | Percent |
|-------|--------|---------|
| Hispanic or Latino: Self-Reported | 47,557,259 | 100.0% |
| Hispanic or Latino by type | | |
| ▸ Mexican | 30,150,333 | 63.4% |
| ▸ Puerto Rican | 4,361,165 | 9.2% |
| ▸ Cuban | 1,696,857 | 3.6% |
| ▸ Dominican | 1,331,495 | 2.8% |
| Central American (excludes Mexicans) | | |
| ▸ Costa Rican | 119,435 | .02% |
| ▸ Guatemalan | 978,539 | 2.0% |
| ▸ Honduran | 588,609 | 1.2% |
| ▸ Nicaraguan | 329,097 | .07% |
| ▸ Panamanian | 153,467 | .03% |
| ▸ Salvadorian | 1,541,272 | 3.5% |
| ▸ Other Central American | 28,438 | —— |
| South American | | |
| ▸ Argentinean | 212,623 | .04% |
| ▸ Bolivian | 93,360 | .01% |
| ▸ Chilean | 120,367 | .02% |
| ▸ Colombian | 864,627 | 1.9% |
| ▸ Ecuadorian | 529,739 | 1.1% |
| ▸ Paraguayan | 18,816 | —— |
| ▸ Peruvian | 503,009 | 1.0% |
| ▸ Uruguayan | 53,470 | .01% |
| ▸ Venezuelan | 204,573 | .04% |
| ▸ Other South American | 19,189 | —— |
| Spaniard | 607,525 | 1.3% |

| Group | Number | Percent |
|---|---|---|
| United States | | |
| Hispanic or Latino Origin by Region | | |
| ▸ Northeast | 6,539,067 | 13.7% |
| ▸ Midwest | 4,431,338 | 9.3% |
| ▸ South | 17,117,750 | 36.0% |
| ▸ West | 19,469,104 | 41.0% |

Source: Adapted from the US Census Bureau (2010).

As cited in Castellano (2011), during the middle passage of the enslaved Africans, fewer than 10 percent were taken to North America. A great majority of the slaves were taken to different places in South America and the Caribbean. Throughout this part of history, Africans mixed with the Native (American) tribes such as the Aztec, Maya, Inca, and Taino. Consequently, one-half of Hispanics' ancestors were already settled when the Europeans, particularly the Spanish, met them. The European ancestry is mostly characterized by Spain's influence and is reflected by Hispanics' most common denominator, the Spanish language. The immigration of individuals to the United States from the Caribbean, Central America, and South America, as well as Spain, continues to impact the already multicultural heritage of Hispanic people. The history of my family (table 3.2) reflects the threefold ancestry with a strong Native American and European (Spain) lineage, along with an African influence.

## Table 3.2: The Castellano Threefold Ancestry

| | Sister | Author as (Brother/Father) | Daughter |
|---|---|---|---|
| Native American | 34% | 34% | 32% |
| Spain (Iberia) | 33% | 28% | 14% |
| Great Britain | 15% | 4% | 15% |
| Italy | 0% | 4% | 25% |
| African | 3% | 2% | 7% |
| West Asian | 7% | 9% | 4% |
| Middle East | 7% | 9% | 0% |
| Scandinavia | 0% | 9% | 0% |
| | 99% | 99% | 97% |

In order to better understand the concept of how Hispanics assimilate into Hispanic Americans, one needs to refer back to the individual countries and their ancestry. Each of these countries boasts the threefold ancestry as previously mentioned. As such, each individual country/territory also has different balances of its ancestry, as well as a completely unique history that has helped shape the culture of its inhabitants. Therefore, each of these countries is unique, and people from these countries are proud of and can distinguish their traditions, customs, clothing, music, dance, and food. The Hispanic presence in almost all areas of community life is most evident through their contributions, rather than their visual identity. It is quite difficult to identify or describe a Hispanic or Latino person based on the way he or she looks. Although there may be certain stereotypes where Hispanics are concerned, these generalizations do not lend themselves to any particular physical characteristic.

According to Darity (2016), 80 percent of third-generation Hispanics are the off-spring of mixed marriages. The consequences, therefore, on Hispanic identification are striking. From one generation to the next, the descendants identify less as Hispanic and more as non-Hispanic white. This trend is referred to as ethnic attrition. A similar preference for whiteness is present among Hispanics who select a single category as their racial identity. The United States Census Bureau (2014) documents that the majority of Hispanic respondents, 53 percent, said they were white, a mere 2.5 percent said they were black, and more than 35 percent chose a category other than black or white. A majority of "single race" Hispanics selected a white racial identity. The census does not include information about an individual's physical appearance. But there are surveys that enable us to compare the interviewees' self-reported race with their complexion as judged by the interviewer. Darity, Dietrich, and Hamilton (2005) developed an interview process devoted exclusively to Hispanics about skin complexion. The interviewers coded the respondents on a continuum of very light, light, medium, dark, and very dark. The vast majority of Hispanics coded as medium to very dark said their race was white. Even among dark and very dark respondents, fewer than 5 percent said they were black. The authors of the study further concluded that the preference for whiteness among Hispanics parallels a flight from blackness.

What does this mean for Hispanic/Latino student identity? In short, it's complicated. There is not one country of Latin America that these students come from, and there is not one code they adhere to. The Hispanic diaspora is unique in that it encompasses people from nineteen different countries and one territory with different histories, immigration experiences, opportunities for education, and life trajectories—each informing how one views the world. This diversity extends from language proficiency to skin color, from socioeconomics to generational status, and from levels of resiliency to identifying with the social trends of the day. The fact is, beyond sharing a common language, Hispanic/Latino students may be the most intraculturally diverse ethnic group in our schools today. However complicated the situation seems to educators or the government, and frustrating to our human need to label and categorize, we must keep in mind that our students are also struggling to understand their own identities. The best way to approach the diversity found among Hispanics is by leaving our own idea of what it means to be Hispanic/Latino behind and empowering the people we meet through affirming how they view themselves.

## Triple Segregation

Hispanic/Latino students are triply segregated in the United States by race, income, and language. The effects of income disparity are discussed in chapter 2, "The Role of Poverty." Here, we will discuss the axis of racial and lingual disparity: names. Names inform identity. I turn when I hear my name called. When my name is called in class, I answer. I used to be bothered when my name was pronounced incorrectly; now, I often make the correct pronunciation into a minilesson that references my ethnicity and related languages. Most of the teachers and professors I had in high school and college could not pronounce my name correctly. I was born Jaime Antonio Castellano (Hi-mĕ On-tonio Kos-te-ya-no). I have been called (Jay-me), (Hi-me), (Hi-knee), and (Hi-men), among others.

For non-Hispanic teachers, pronouncing a student's name correctly provides that student with validation, authenticity, and a sense of belonging. In terms of cross-cultural communication and understanding, the correct pronunciation of names can help teachers on their way to building positive relationships with students and also serve as a springboard to promoting academic achievement. Mitchell (2016) writes that My Name, My Identity is a national campaign that places a premium on pronouncing students' names correctly and valuing diversity and is a partnership between the National Association for Bilingual Education (NABE), the Santa Clara County Office of Education, and the California Association for Bilingual Education. It focuses on the fact that a student's name is more than what he or she is called—it's the foundation of who he or she is. It's one of the first things children recognize, it's one of the first words they learn to say, and it's how the world identifies them. For students, especially the children of immigrants or those who are ELLs, a teacher who knows their name and can pronounce it correctly signals respect and marks a critical step in helping them adjust to school. For many Hispanics and ELLs, a mispronounced name is often the first of many slights they experience in classrooms; they're already unlikely to see educators who are like them, teachers who speak their language, or a curriculum that reflects their culture.

The solution is as easy as asking a student the correct pronunciation of his or her name. There must be a desire to want to know, a desire to build a classroom community by building bridges and making connections with students. As a teacher, principal, and administrator who is also Spanish-speaking, I have had countless numbers of Hispanic students tell me I was the first educator to pronounce their name correctly. This was huge in creating nurturing and respectful relationships with them. The national campaign goes on to ask: What about you? Are you the kind of educator who makes a conscious effort to pronounce student names correctly, or do you laugh it off when you make a mistake? Do you validate students by asking them about pronunciation, or do you comment as to why their name is so difficult to pronounce? How would you pronounce the following names?

- Jermanie
- Matìas
- Nicolás
- Junibei

- Kenielys
- Keyshaneilys
- Adelaida
- Osleidys

- Magaly
- Soraida
- Zulerqui
- Rigoberto

On a scale of one to ten, with one being "I missed them all" and ten being "I pronounced all of them correctly," how did you do? As educators, we cannot be afraid of failure. If it is embarrassing to try to pronounce these names with the correct accents and emphases, imagine how it feels for the student to continuously hear a foundational part of his or her identity dismissed as being too complicated. Nicholas is not the same student as Nicolás, and both students deserve to be recognized.

Roberts (2016) reports that Hispanic births and immigration have led to Hispanic surnames being among the most popular and that six of the fifteen most common surnames in the United States were of Hispanic origin in 2010, compared to four of fifteen in 2000, and none as recently as 1990. Smith, Johnson, Williams, Brown, and Jones still remain the most common of the 6.3 million last names reported in 2010, but Garcia had edged up from eighth to sixth, closing in on Jones and Brown. The ascendency of the Hispanic names reflects both the surge of immigrants from Latin America over the past several decades and the fact that Hispanic surnames tend to be less diverse. Garcia and Rodriguez were joined in the top ten in 2010 by Martinez (the fifteen most popular also include Hernandez).

**1990 Top 15 Surnames:**

| | | |
|---|---|---|
| 1. Smith | 6. Davis | 11. Anderson |
| 2. Johnson | 7. Miller | 12. Thomas |
| 3. Williams | 8. Wilson | 13. Jackson |
| 4. Jones | 9. Moore | 14. White |
| 5. Brown | 10. Taylor | 15. Harris |

**2000 Top 15 Surnames:**

| | | |
|---|---|---|
| 1. Smith | 6. Miller | 11. **Martinez** |
| 2. Johnson | 7. Davis | 12. Anderson |
| 3. Williams | 8. **Garcia** | 13. Taylor |
| 4. Jones | 9. **Rodriguez** | 14. Thomas |
| 5. Brown | 10. Wilson | 15. **Hernandez** |

**2010 Top 15 Surnames:**

| | | |
|---|---|---|
| 1. Smith | 6. **Garcia** | 11. **Hernandez** |
| 2. Johnson | 7. Miller | 12. **Lopez** |
| 3. Williams | 8. Davis | 13. **Gonzalez** |
| 4. Jones | 9. **Rodriguez** | 14. Wilson |
| 5. Brown | 10. **Martinez** | 15. Anderson |

Hispanic/Latino names in every classroom are only going to become more common. Teachers who put themselves out there for their students are offering the first steps of a relationship built on trust and respect.

## Balancing School, Family, and Community

When one looks at the complex cross section of Hispanic/Latino students attending our nation's public schools, academic achievement data help us identify how these students are performing in core content areas. These assessments do not account for how students feel, if they have been fed, or the fact that many Hispanic/Latino students live in a world of conflict and contradiction and are put in situations where navigating their lives is difficult and demanding. This conflicting world in which these students live is accompanied by a range of social and emotional behaviors that can manipulate, or influence, how they react in school. The code-switching between their classes, their peers, and their families can have a significant effect on their identity.

### In Class

According to Castellano (2011), many of these students, even those identified as gifted, advanced, or high-ability, are often overwhelmed by the mixed messages they are given by those individuals and institutions that are part of their daily reality. First, we have the institutional culture of the school that is driven by such democratic principles as following rules, taking turns, speaking when spoken to, respecting others, and demonstrating behaviors promoting good citizenship. In this environment, we pledge allegiance to the flag, may sing the national anthem, and follow a plethora of rules and regulations designed to establish order. Instruction is almost always in English, and English is what students are expected to speak. Traditional ideas of politeness and deference to authority figures, often white teachers, are strongly enforced.

## In the Neighborhood

The democratic expectations of the school are often in conflict with the socialized environment that many of our Hispanic/Latino students face on a daily basis. That is, the "street life" and peer groups of these students often take precedence over doing well in school. In this socialized environment, survival is the key. Many feel a familial bond to their peer group, where the pressure to fit in, either through intimidation or expectation, is simply too great. A mixture of spoken Spanish and English is common, almost always in a less formal dialect. Respect is centered on influential members of the neighborhood, and for students living in areas with severe gang violence, deference to these figures can be a matter of life and death. As a result, many do not realize their true potential during the traditional school day.

## In the Home

A third world that many Hispanic/Latino students must contend with is that of the home, which at times is in competition with the expectations of both the school and the community. For many Hispanic/Latino students, their parents want their children to honor and respect tradition, culture, religion, and language, all while maintaining ties to the old ways. A more formal Spanish is commonly spoken, with the accent and idioms of the family's heritage country. In many Hispanic/Latino homes, the family is expected to come first; some may even expect their child to assist the family first by working over going to school. These students are being pulled in multiple directions and are caught in a sociocultural tug-of-war (Castellano, 2011). When having to contend with this level of incongruence, school may not have the greatest importance or relevance. Table 3.3 summarizes these factors.

Students may feel they are a different person in different groups. Code-switching between formal English, informal Spanglish, and formal Spanish between school, the community, and at home can influence this feeling of identity fracturing. Schools can help to lower the barrier Hispanic/Latino students face in trying to engage with and prioritize their learning by providing instruction in the language they are most comfortable speaking.

## Learning in Spanish

In the American public school system, Hispanic students who are non-English- or limited-English-speaking are considered limited English proficient (LEP), the official label designated by the US Department of Education. However, they are more commonly referred to as English language learners (ELLs). During the 2013–2014

Table 3.3: Balancing Home, School, and Community Worlds

| Why Hispanic/Latino Students Do Less Well in School | | |
|---|---|---|
| **The Home** | **The School** | **The Community** |
| ▸ Poverty<br>▸ Poor nutrition<br>▸ Domestic violence<br>▸ Alcoholic parent<br>▸ Drug-addicted parent<br>▸ Drugs<br>▸ Abuse (physical, sexual, emotional)<br>▸ Neglect<br>▸ Parents with limited education<br>▸ Emphasis on language, culture, heritage<br>▸ Lack of health insurance<br>▸ Inadequate housing<br>▸ Overcrowding | ▸ Expectation to conform; rules applied inconsistently<br>▸ Ineffective teachers who have given up or don't care<br>▸ Social and emotional needs of students are ignored<br>▸ Cultural, racial conflicts<br>▸ Cultural stereotypes (poor students are intellectually inferior)<br>▸ Poor leadership<br>▸ Lack of cross-cultural communication and understanding<br>▸ Limited resources<br>▸ Lowered expectations<br>▸ Teachers and leaders not culturally competent<br>▸ Schooling not relevant<br>▸ Overcrowding<br>▸ No after-school programs offered | ▸ Influence of the peer group<br>▸ Drugs<br>▸ Gangs<br>▸ Violence<br>▸ Lack of social services<br>▸ Racial, cultural, linguistic discrimination<br>▸ Unemployment<br>▸ Underemployment<br>▸ Social injustice<br>▸ Fear of deportation<br>▸ Inadequate housing<br>▸ No after-school programs offered |

school year, nearly 5 million ELLs attended US public and secondary schools; the ELL population represents slightly more than 10 percent of the nation's K–12 student population. With 3.8 million students listing Spanish as their home language, about three out of every four ELLs in US schools are Spanish-speakers. The biggest growth in ELLs in the United States is taking place in rural and suburban school systems, according to Rix (2010). The ELL population has been growing steadily for well over a decade, and if the growth trend continues, it is expected to double by 2025. I have witnessed firsthand what happens when teachers and administrators do not understand their racially, culturally, and increasingly linguistically diverse students. These students become disenfranchised, disillusioned, and believe that teachers and administrators do not care about them.

The Migration Policy Institute of the National Center on Immigrant Integration Policy (2015a) reports that in terms of size of ELL population, California, Florida,

Texas, New York, Illinois, Colorado, Washington, and North Carolina each have more than 100,000 ELLs. Together, these eight states account for more than two-thirds of the nation's ELL enrollment in public schools. At the local level, twenty-five school districts (table 3.4) accounted for nearly one-quarter (23 percent) of all ELLs in K–12 public schools in 2011–2012. California had the highest concentration of ELLs in the United States, and not surprisingly, nearly one-third of the country's districts with the largest ELL populations (eight of twenty-five districts) were found in California. With enrollment of more than 150,000 ELLs, the Los Angeles Unified School District had the largest ELL population (152,592 students), closely followed by New York City (142,572). Each of these two districts had higher ELL enrollments than the next two largest districts combined: Nevada's Clark County School District (68,577) and Florida's Miami-Dade County School District (66,497). The majority of these school districts were located within states that have been traditional immigrant destinations, but several districts in new immigrant destination states also ranked in the country's top twenty-five ELL enrollment districts. This includes Fairfax County Public Schools in Virginia (36,551), Montgomery County Public Schools in Maryland (20,580), and Gwinnett County Public Schools in Georgia (18,968). What this means is that ELLs will continue to increase as Hispanic/Latino student populations increase. Every state in this country has ELLs, and every district needs to be aware of how far-reaching this population is.

**Table 3.4: Top 25 School Districts by ELL Enrollment, 2011–2012**

| District/Agency Name | State | ELL Enrollment | Total K–12 Enrollment | Share of ELLs among K–12 Students (%) |
|---|---|---|---|---|
| Los Angeles Unified | CA | 152,592 | 659,639 | 23.1 |
| New York City | NY | 142,572 | 968,143 | 14.7 |
| Clark County | NV | 68,577 | 313,398 | 21.9 |
| Miami-Dade County | FL | 66,497 | 350,239 | 19.0 |
| Dallas Independent | TX | 56,650 | 157,575 | 36.0 |
| Houston Independent | TX | 54,333 | 203,066 | 26.8 |
| City of Chicago | IL | 53,786 | 403,004 | 13.3 |
| Fairfax County | VA | 36,551 | 177,606 | 20.6 |
| San Diego Unified | CA | 36,453 | 131,044 | 27.8 |
| Santa Ana Unified | CA | 32,170 | 57,250 | 56.2 |
| Orange County | FL | 28,311 | 180,000 | 15.7 |
| SD 1: County of Denver | CO | 25,417 | 80,890 | 31.4 |

| District/Agency Name | State | ELL Enrollment | Total K–12 Enrollment | Share of ELLs among K–12 Students (%) |
|---|---|---|---|---|
| Hawaii Dept. of Education | HI | 24,750 | 182,706 | 13.5 |
| Broward County | FL | 24,143 | 258,478 | 9.3 |
| Hillsborough County | FL | 22,474 | 197,041 | 11.4 |
| Fort Worth Independent | TX | 21,913 | 83,109 | 26.4 |
| Austin Independent | TX | 21,751 | 86,528 | 25.1 |
| Long Beach Unified | CA | 20,746 | 83,691 | 24.8 |
| Garden Grove Unified | CA | 20,743 | 47,999 | 43.2 |
| Montgomery County | MD | 20,580 | 146,459 | 14.1 |
| Gwinnett County | GA | 18,968 | 162,370 | 11.7 |
| Palm Beach County | FL | 18,698 | 176,901 | 10.6 |
| Fresno Unified | CA | 17,536 | 74,235 | 23.6 |
| San Bernardino Unified | CA | 17,488 | 54,379 | 32.2 |
| San Francisco Unified | CA | 17,083 | 56,310 | 30.3 |

*Source: Migration Policy Institute (2015a).*

The Migration Policy Institute (2015a) further reports that with the exception of Hawaii, the top language spoken by ELLs in the remaining twenty-four districts is Spanish (in Hawaii, the language most spoken by its ELLs is Ilokano). They also document that in forty-five states and the District of Columbia more than two-thirds of ELLs spoke Spanish as their home language. Language is such an integral part of a person's identity; it shapes how we think, our perception of the world, and how we connect to our heritage. Hundreds of thousands of our students are learning in a language they are not fluent in, a language they may feel few cultural connections to, and a language they identify with harsh political rhetoric instead of the safety and comfort of home. Schools can bridge the gap between the security of Spanish and the foreignness of English by engaging in dual-language strategies.

The College Board offers hope to those ELLs who are college bound by offering, for the first time in 2016, testing accommodations that include translated instructions, additional time, and having instructions read to them. In the classroom, teachers can offer this same hope in a variety of ways:

- Use alternate seating patterns.
  - Keep ELLs close to the teacher's desk for easy access.
  - Identify high-performing or bilingual students who may volunteer to be buddies with an ELL and seat them together.

- Make the content comprehensible.
  - Use visuals and props to illustrate a point; account for different learning styles.
  - Incorporate technology like computer games and simulations.
- Monitor tone and teacher talk.
  - Take the time to speak clearly and enunciate.
  - Rephrase academic language/vocabulary.
  - Keep the tone conversational rather than dogmatic.
  - Be open to questions.
- Modify assignments.
  - Allow ELLs to write one paragraph instead of two.
  - Make questions or prompts relevant to the students.
  - Account for fewer spelling words to master or supplement spelling tests with Spanish words.
- Reinforce social and academic language.
  - Initiate a word wall and/or grammar wall. As a trainer and coach of middle school teachers serving a large ELL population, I encouraged them to use this strategy to reinforce both language types. The process was authentic as the additions to both types of walls would come from the students themselves.

A final critical step educators must take to empower their ELLs is to be an advocate for bilingualism. For students who are bullied for their limited use of English, isolated from both casual conversations and political dialogue, and subject to ridicule for their accents in pop culture, being bilingual can seem like a burden rather than a blessing. Though America has no official language, English proficiency is assessed during citizenship exams and is unarguably the mainstream default. For students who identify more as an American than with their heritage country, Spanish becomes a reminder of all the ways they are different. But the research of Marian and Shook (2015) documents that there are explicit cognitive benefits of being bilingual. Among the benefits is that bilingualism has been associated with improved metalinguistic awareness (ability to recognize language as a system that can be manipulated and explored), better memory, better visual-spatial skills, and even more creativity. Furthermore, beyond these cognitive advantages, there are also valuable social benefits that come from being bilingual, among them the ability to explore a culture through its native tongue or talk to someone with whom you might otherwise never be able to communicate.

By advocating these advantages, schools can help reverse the stigma that comes with being an ELL and instead encourage all students to become bilingual.

## Culture in the Classroom

Increased dual-language learning opens the door to the most effective strategy for making schools an integral and positive aspect of a Hispanic/Latino student's sense of identity: increased Hispanic/Latino cultural representation in the classroom. As our collective understanding increases about Hispanic/Latino students, our knowledge of their unique characteristics and cultural backgrounds can be made a part of classroom culture. An ethnic studies approach can be integrated into any lesson of any subject because it relies on a simple premise: rather than teach all students based on the same Eurocentric techniques and examples, teachers should instead use subject matter relevant to their unique students. Providing curriculum resources that portray Hispanic/Latino ethnicity and heritage allows for students to explore the intersection of their identity and academics. Put another way, when students can see people who look like them and/or come from their situation or who represent part of their culture in the context of learning and success, they begin to see themselves in that context. More and more school districts across the United States are beginning to discover the importance of addressing the needs of Hispanic/Latino students through a delivery model that demonstrates integrity and respect for their ethnic, cultural, and linguistic diversity.

How do teachers incorporate Hispanic/Latino culture without coming off as patronizing, appropriating, or insincere? Step one in programming for the success of Hispanic/Latino students is to build positive, meaningful relationships with them. When students know who you are and trust that you want to know who they are, they are willing to team up with you to achieve academic success. In all my years of teaching, following are the factors that have allowed me to connect with my students.

- **Be authentic; be real:** Even at very young ages, students know the difference between a teacher who is authentic and one who is simply going through the motions. Acknowledging victories and struggles is part of relationship building. The authentic teacher asks the students questions when unsure; victories are celebrated together, and struggles become problem-solving opportunities.

- **Empathize:** The journey toward cultural competency includes empathy, the ability to share the feelings of another. And because each student comes to school with his or her own personal story, it is important to be attentive to and understanding of his or her individual perspectives. By practicing empathy, a teacher looks at a given situation through a different lens as clarification and seeks meaning.

- **Adopt a personal commitment:** Showing students that you care about them helps break down barriers and unlock their potential. A personal commitment to your Hispanic/Latino students should also include sharing values, beliefs, and attitudes with parents and families. The more you discover about your students' day-to-day living realities, the more likely you are to honor their voices in demonstrating what they know and are able to do.

- **Administer brief informal surveys and questionnaires:** Polling students on any number of topics allows teachers to capture meaningful information and data that can strategically inform curriculum, instruction, and assessment. During the first week of every school year, I encourage my teachers to administer an interest inventory and learning style inventory to their students. The information obtained further allows teachers to build positive relationships with their students.

- **Create a safe, nurturing classroom:** A safe, nurturing classroom is one that values and honors each student's unique learning style and cultural and linguistic background and provides opportunities to grow academically, cognitively, socially, and emotionally. In these classrooms, a "liberated zone" is created whereby students will not be judged and where they can take risks without being ridiculed, laughed at, or thought of as different.

- **Be observant:** Teachers who are observant and notice the little things that make each of their students different from one another are quicker to build positive, meaningful relationships with them. Observant teachers realize they may share a common interest or some common characteristic with a student and use it as a way to motivate, engage, and connect with him or her.

- **Create fluid, flexible groupings:** Teachers who understand the academic strengths and challenges of their students are able to make adjustments through intentional grouping arrangements that are fluid and flexible. This approach allows for personalized learning that capitalizes on the potential that each student has. Learn more about this in Fluid Teaching in chapter 4.

A teacher is most effective when he or she becomes a trusted mentor instead of just an instructor. Making your classroom a team means the students have faith in you. Validate their trust by demonstrating cultural competency and responsive pedagogy.

- **Invite guest speakers:** Identify relevant partners from the community who have achieved success and understand the challenges these students face.

- **Plant a garden:** Plant food types common in many Spanish-speaking countries, such as corn, beans, squash, and peppers. Have students keep a log tracking the growth of the various plants. Encourage them to use charts, graphs, and art in reporting information. Extend the project by researching staple foods of other regions.

+ **Saca tu bandera (raise your flag):** Give students the opportunity to supplement their learning by sharing the flag of their country of origin and telling stories about their family's background. As a principal of an elementary school with a large Hispanic population, I placed the flags of all nineteen Spanish-speaking nations and one territory in the main office. It created a welcoming atmosphere and allowed parents and families to immediately identify with the child's school.

+ **Celebrate mi familia (my family):** Allow students to bring in photos of their family, culture, customs, dress, food, heritage country, and such. Allow them to share their story with classmates. The end result is a class mural that celebrates diversity, inclusion, and family.

+ **Recognize heroes:** Give students the opportunity to research someone in their family, from the community, or a historical figure from their country of origin/ethnicity and to share this information with classmates through writing, art, and/or technology.

+ **Create a timeline:** Track the contributions of Hispanics/Latinos to the United States and the world by creating a timeline that includes the individual's name, country of origin, national flag, and contribution. Challenge students to create a timeline that goes all around the classroom.

Celebrating and honoring the diversity of students is important to their social and emotional growth and development. Creating and supporting an inclusive, culturally rich classroom creates an environment that respects and honors the diversity of all learners. Using engaging, motivating, and focused instruction by including students' cultural strengths and referencing their specific ethnicity in the teaching and learning process is the most effective way to help students understand and assimilate content knowledge. Even more important than helping them meet rubric goals, incorporating an ethnic studies approach to teaching allows minority and disadvantaged students to visualize themselves as learners, entrepreneurs, and history makers. By bringing their culture into the classroom, we make success part of their identity.

## Conclusion

Classrooms across our nation's public schools are filled with Hispanic/Latino students. Although they share a common origin and linguistic base, the groups that make up the Hispanic/Latino population are not monolithic, as they differ significantly in many important ways. Successful retention of this complex cross section of intra-ethnic diversity is incumbent on the supporting infrastructure of the school and district—inclusionary beliefs, attitudes, practices, and procedures. Moreover, the programs and services offered to Hispanic/Latino students should reflect institutional policies and practices that document the system's commitment to principles of equity and access. Each is inextricably linked with the other. Schools and districts that are proactive in these areas most likely have a dynamic program that reflects the demographic of the school and are cognizant of the specific Hispanic/Latino ethnicities of the school community. They embrace cultural, ethnic, and linguistic diversity and engage in behaviors that validate pluralism, multiculturalism, and cultural competency.

The diversity found in our Hispanic/Latino students reinforces the belief that one size does not fit all. All students are attempting to forge their unique identity, but for Hispanic/Latino students, this can be even more challenging. Educators who are informed about how their students identify themselves and what languages they are most comfortable learning in can avoid triply segregating them from their peers. Furthermore, by incorporating cultural examples that are relevant to the demographics of your school, teachers can prevent education from becoming a negative participant in the tug-of-war Hispanic/Latino students face from their family and community. When schools acknowledge and validate student identities, they build bridges of trust that can lead to success for all their students.

# CHAPTER 4

# Opening the Doors to Hope, Promise, and Possibility

> At seventeen years of age, he left his Mexican barrio to attend a state university. As the fourth of five siblings, he was the first to go to college. It was a big deal in his barrio, and everyone had high hopes that he would be successful and serve as a role model for his siblings and other kids in the barrio. His mother, sisters, aunts, uncles, and grandmother made the two-hour trip to his new home, Lincoln Hall, an on-campus dormitory for male students. He left home with one suitcase and a monthly allowance of $25 that came in the form of financial aid. He was afraid but did not show it. After the final goodbyes, he sat alone in his dorm room terrified of what was ahead. The dorm floor housed fifty young men; he was the only non-white. He had never gone to school with white kids before. His new roommate was from one of Chicago's wealthy suburbs, and it was clear he was disappointed he would be sharing a room with someone who was not white. The racial taunting was immediate. Vaseline was smeared on his room's doorknob; his toiletries were stolen while he was in the shower; "Mexicans go home" and other such notes were routinely found under his door. Most guys on his floor ignored him. The racism, prejudice, and discrimination he experienced disappointed him but did not break him. He demonstrated the resiliency and perseverance often characteristic of survivors. He became friends with three or four guys who did not care that he was Mexican, poor, and from the barrio. They advocated for him, ate meals with him, and spent time with him during the weekends. There were very few Hispanic/Latino students at this university. Those he met often faced the same racism, prejudice, and discrimination as him. They banded together to support one another and to survive. He was also smart enough to join an on-campus student organization called OLAS (Organization of Latin American Students). This network of support helped him adjust, make

Continued →

new friends, and establish an infrastructure of support, and they accepted him as he was. He decided that he would not allow ignorant racist individuals to prevent him from getting an education and fulfilling his dream of becoming a teacher.    **"**

The disturbing reality is that since the advent of norm-referenced assessments that compare student subgroups, Hispanic/Latino students, as a group, have always hovered in the bottom quartile—always! And despite hundreds of millions of dollars, billions even, being poured into school reform and improvement efforts, government takeover of schools, and conversion to charter schools, Hispanic/Latino students—although making great strides in high school graduation rates, gaining increased access to advanced academic programs, and through bilingual education being allowed to speak, read, and write in the Spanish language—remain in the national conversation as one of the lowest achieving of all student groups, along with their African American and Native American classmates. Hispanic/Latino students are not pariahs but rather a rich, untapped national resource and treasure. The conundrum becomes how to best actualize their talent and potential, despite their zip code, skin color, ethnicity, and socioeconomic status. The consequence for taking no action is simply too frightening to fathom. In other words, we are in a race between education and catastrophe. In the pages that follow, the reader will be taken on a journey that plants seeds of hope, inspiration, and commitment and given exposure to new perspectives, strategies, and ideas.

## No Excuses

The first, most critical part of this chapter is acknowledging reality: there is a significant achievement gap between our Hispanic/Latino students and other student populations. Olszewski-Kubilius and Clarenbach (2012) write that the term *achievement gap* typically has been used to refer to disparities between subgroups of students reaching minimal levels of achievement compared to their white counterparts. Research by Plucker, Giancola, Healy, et al. (2015) indicates that these gaps exist at every level of achievement, including at the very top levels. Hispanics/Latinos and ELLs are severely underrepresented among the top 1 percent, 5 percent, and 10 percent of all students at all levels of the education system, from prekindergarten through graduate and professional school. A major reason for these achievement gaps is that many more Hispanic (32 percent) children live in low-socioeconomic circumstances compared to Asian (14 percent) and white children (17 percent). Sixty percent of the five million ELLs in the United States qualify for the free and reduced-price lunch program. The "No excuses; I don't see color or poverty" professional learning mentality is not acceptable for an educator attempting to promote equity, access, and opportunity in his or her classroom. Not all students enter the classroom on equal footing. Disregarding the internal struggles these kids face does not make them better students; it makes us worse educators. The first step to solving a problem is recognizing that you have one. How can we begin to address the unique needs of Hispanic/Latino students until we are comfortable with acknowledging the effects of undocumented immigration, poverty, and identity politics?

I was a school-based executive director of a Spanish/English dual-language immersion charter school program that followed a 50/50 bilingual education model; each grade level had the same number of English- and Spanish-speaking teachers. Half of each day was spent learning in English, the other half-day in Spanish. This model attracted a dichotomy of parents and students. On one hand, our white students were the sons and daughters of doctors, lawyers, university professors, scholars, CEOs, and the like. On the other hand, our Hispanic/Latino students qualified us for Title I; they were the sons and daughters of laborers, migrants, factory workers, and parents who hovered in poverty. The school experienced much success. However, approximately 25 percent of the faculty and staff would often comment about the diversity of the school and claim that they did not see the poverty of our Hispanic/Latino students or the dark colors of their skin. Part of becoming a culturally competent teacher is understanding the impact of poverty on students and accepting those facts. Part of becoming a culturally competent teacher is recognizing the great diversity found within the Hispanic/Latino diaspora, embracing it, and finding ways in teaching and learning that allow these students to feel pride about who they are and where they come from. If they did not see poverty or color, what did they see?

During one professional development day, I put all of the teachers on a bus and drove through the various communities where our Hispanic/Latino students lived. We returned to the school and continued our training looking at the numbers, data in the form of our Title I budget, the number of students on free and reduced-price lunch, and disaggregated and compared achievement data. This journey was an eye-opener for some. Through courageous conversations, self-assessments, and reflection on practices, I could actually see and hear the transformation that took place. It was incredible!

Teachers and administrators who do not see color or poverty are denying who these students are and where they come from. What they need are teachers and administrators who are culturally competent and empathetic, who employ culturally responsive instruction, and who build community through forming relationships and using effective cross-cultural communication and understanding. Ultimately the "no excuses" professional learning mentality only serves as an excuse for low-achieving educators to dismiss students rather than empower them. To seal the achievement gap, we must acknowledge it exists—and not as a function of how our students react to their circumstances but as a function of how educators fail to respond to their needs.

## Professionalization

Countries with a model education system value their teachers. The Network for Public Education (2016) reports that many of the popular American reforms give lip service to the professionalization of teaching while displaying an appalling lack of understanding of what professionalization truly means. Teachers are viewed as interchangeable, and experience is discounted, even viewed as a flaw. Courses that provide potential teachers with a deep understanding of the history of the profession, learning theory, or cognitive development are regarded as fluff. Instead, current reforms promote online teacher preparation and on-the-job training and summer training that push inexperienced young people, with inadequate preparation, into classrooms. Yet, research tells us that fast-track teacher preparation and licensure programs serve to lower professional status. One of the first discussions I have with my undergraduate preservice teacher candidates is about professionalization and what that means to them. To me, professionalization is characterized by cultural competency, professional development, and caring.

### Cultural Competency

From an instructional perspective, teachers and administrators who are culturally competent and use culturally responsive pedagogy ensure that students feel physiologically, socially, and emotionally safe and secure, in part, by using textbooks, resources, and materials in which students see themselves represented. As discussed in chapter 3, when teachers are intentional in their use of classroom space and equipment to create an inclusive and relevant environment, students are able to become effectively engaged in learning. Cultural competency means practicing restorative justice rather than zero tolerance, ensuring that students do not lose instructional time, that they are kept in school and supported by counselors, teachers, or administrators, as opposed to being suspended or expelled. For some Hispanic/Latino students, school is where they learn about the importance of discipline, routine, and structure.

Schools as institutions can also practice cultural competency by hiring minority educators and administrators. With Hispanic/Latino students now accounting for 25 percent of all students, offering opportunities for different cultural and ethnic voices to join in the conversation is more important than ever. In a document titled *The State of Racial Diversity in the Educator Workforce*, the US Department of Education's Office of Planning, Evaluation, and Policy Development (2016) reports that while students of color are expected to make up 56 percent of the student population by 2024, the elementary and secondary educator workforce is still overwhelmingly white. In fact, the most recent US Department of Education School and Staffing Survey (SASS), a nationally representative survey of teachers and principals, shows that in its 2015–2016 survey, 80 percent of public school teachers identified as white.

**2015–2016 Survey of Racial Diversity of Teachers**

- 80% of public school teachers were white

- 9% of public school teachers were Hispanic

- 7% of public school teachers were black

- 2% of public school teachers were Asian

- 1% of public school teachers were American Indian or Alaska Native

- 77% of teachers were women

- 90% of elementary school teachers were women

This 80 percent figure has hardly changed in more than fifteen years; data from a similar survey conducted by the department in 2000 found that 84 percent of teachers identified as white. Generally speaking, Hispanic/Latino students in the United States are being taught by white females. Having a diverse teaching force can be a valuable resource for all learners, not only for Hispanic/Latino students. A variety of perspectives enriches every aspect of the learning community.

Culturally competent teachers and administrators who "get it" when working with Hispanic/Latino students put themselves in a position to make a difference based on their ability to use relational pedagogy, which here means the use of instructional processes, strategies, and activities that promote both increased academic achievement and mastery of learning, as well as having a connection that empowers and encourages students to include any element of their culture, ethnicity, or language in demonstrating what they know and are able to do.

When used effectively, teachers and administrators are able to develop a warm, positive, supportive, and responsive relationship with each student and help each student learn about and take pride in his or her individual and cultural identity. According to the Institute for Educational Leadership (2005), culturally competent leaders link cultural competency and relational pedagogy to effectiveness, equitable opportunities for students, and a positive, accepting school environment. Multicultural education also allows teachers and administrators to examine a variety of strategies that employ culturally responsive pedagogy and involve parents, families, and communities. Intersecting multicultural education with instructional pedagogy includes an intentional focus on curriculum, instruction, assessment, individualized learning, differentiation, the use of support teams, and the use of data for planning purposes. Winebrenner (2001) adds that teachers and administrators should:

- Discover and acknowledge what students already know

- Engage and guide them in planning projects that capitalize on their interests

- Allow them flexibility in the way they use their time
- Allow them to learn at different rates
- Help them to be aware of and use productive learning strategies
- Provide a balance of skill-building and meaning-making activities
- Plan a variety of reality-based learning experiences in which the students monitor the effectiveness of their behaviors
- Teach them to be self-sufficient
- Encourage them to demonstrate mastery in a wide variety of ways

Educators can best achieve these ideals by improving their cultural competency, a foundational aspect of connecting emotionally with students and building a relationship based on trust. Cultural competency is a state of mind that moves beyond conventional wisdom, assumptions, and traditional constructs of how we view others. It begins with the individual engaged in a process of revelation and truth about "who I am" and "what I know" about myself and my relationships with others. The expectation is that the adults in the school affirm a deeper appreciation of diversity and are able to respond to and develop meaningful relationships with their students. These interpersonal relationships may also serve as a template for students as they forge their own relationships with others both in and outside the school.

Teachers and administrators who are not culturally competent cannot be fully effective because they have yet to understand their own personal biases and cultural values.

## Professional Development

Professional development means teachers recognize that receiving their degree is only the beginning of the learning process. Feedback and professional training should be integral aspects of an educator's career.

Feedback is the process of giving and receiving coaching. Coaching to support teachers and administrators with instruction and instructional leadership involves observations, providing explicit feedback through conferencing, and becoming a resource person and resource provider. A coach facilitates experiences through team planning and collaboration, allowing the individual to find his or her voice and have his or her say. Modeling effective and culturally responsive pedagogy is part of the coaching-to-support model.

Coaching to inspire and motivate involves the use of positive reinforcement, detailing what teachers and administrators are doing well and encouraging them to continue using what works. All such praise must revolve around practices and processes that support student learning. Much like we do with students, acknowledging the hard work of teachers and administrators is part of the coaching-to-inspire-and-motivate model.

Coaching to improve involves being honest and truthful about what has been observed. Here, the coach serves as a resource person, helping teachers and administrators identify missed opportunities and guiding them to what could be done differently in the future. The focus is always on instruction and instructional leadership that supports student learning. Sharing expertise and suggestions for improving instruction is another example of how they are a resource person in the coaching-to-improve model.

Every teacher and administrator in a school has the ability to be a coach for his or her colleagues. The process of giving and taking critiques and advice ensures that the school functions together as a community of instructors and learners. Here are some tips on how to give and take the most effective feedback:

- Consider tone and body language when giving and receiving feedback. In both formative and summative evaluations, I would always sit next to the teacher and use a steady and confident tone of voice. I found that this helped teachers be more comfortable.

- After a brief welcome and perhaps some small talk, I would make it a point to clearly communicate the purpose of the evaluation and the desired outcome before providing feedback. Teachers often expressed appreciation that by the end of our time together the results of the evaluation gave them peace of mind. They would not have to continue their day in suspense, not knowing.

- Being explicit and concise kept the meeting on track. The use of "I statements" as opposed to using general terms kept the process at a professional level. In receiving feedback, the teachers were able to follow up with clarifying questions because we both used the language emphasized in the evaluation. Being concise and explicit helps eliminate any sense of subjectivity.

- Begin and end an evaluation with positive feedback. This was an intentional behavior on my part, designed to build authentic relationships with teachers that also made them feel good about themselves.

- Reciprocal feedback also gives teachers an opportunity to share their voice and have their say in the evaluation process. I would say something like, "Would you like to share any feedback with me about anything that we talked about or the information that I shared?" This intentional invitation allowed teachers to practice the very skill they need for giving and receiving feedback to and from students.

Professional training involves taking that feedback and learning how to improve on it through individual or group learning sessions. Such training can occur via formal in-services, regularly scheduled staff meetings, communications with staff, or external professional development opportunities (e.g., conferences, workshops). These opportunities should be woven into traditional school tasks and not seen as add-ons. Most important, they should never stop. For as long as we are teaching, we should also be learning. In a school culture of personal growth and development, there is also an acknowledgment and acceptance that teachers and administrators can move between readiness levels based on their experiences, education, research, and willingness to self-identify on any given topic. This fluidity ensures that they get the most out of their professional learning experiences. Empowering teachers and administrators with the tools they need to be effective in educating Hispanic/Latino students leads them to improved student performance and connectedness.

With improving cultural competency in mind, professional learning opportunities for teachers and administrators can focus on gaining a greater understanding about the history, values, beliefs, and perspectives of people from different cultural backgrounds. Understanding and acknowledging local demographics informs which of the twenty Hispanic/Latino ethnicities should be focused on.

## Caring

Quantitatively, and historically, there are benchmarks for professionalism in the form of earned degrees, teaching licenses, transcripts, and acquired certifications that serve as documentation stating one is qualified. Caring, on the other hand, is a qualitative construct and means different things to different people. Ideally, caring teachers nurture, support, challenge, engage, inspire, and motivate their students. They collaborate with parents and families, and they are intentional in their efforts to make a positive difference in the lives of the students they serve. The challenge for any principal and human resources department is to identify and hire teachers who are both caring and qualified. A caring educator embraces diversity by being respectful, inquisitive, and authentic. Educators who are both qualified and caring have the best chance to be successful when working with students who are low-income and racially, culturally, and linguistically diverse. Most Hispanic/Latino students attend public school, live in poverty, and qualify for free or reduced-price lunch. Teachers and administrators who care enough to put in the work needed to help this intra-ethnically diverse group of students reach their greatest chance of success must be better able to adjust the teaching-learning processes to promote academic, social, and emotional growth and development in their students than their counterparts who do not have the same passion and empathy.

We've discussed promoting equity, access, and opportunity for all students. Professional teachers apply these principles to every stakeholder, including themselves and their fellow teachers. Does every teacher in your school have access to the same resources and opportunities to further himself or herself as an educator? Is anyone left out of development seminars or sidelined from cultural discussions? Are there some community groups your school refuses to work with? Caring means you look to encourage parent involvement, teacher involvement, and community involvement to gain the most student involvement.

Professionalization of teaching is an ongoing process. Even an "expert" teacher may find himself or herself at a lower readiness level depending on the year and composition of his or her classroom. Where are you right now, and where do you want to be a week from now, a month from now, a year from now? The following categories are designed to stimulate thought and action while pursuing individualized professional growth and development.

### The Novice

1. Define cultural proficiency, including key characteristics of culturally responsive schools.

2. Reflect on one's own viewpoints and biases, including the role that personal and family histories and group memberships play in the formation of these identities.

3. Review daily routines, the calendar, and your commitment to family and friends and determine how ready you are to invest in your classroom and students.

4. Identify one professional development opportunity beyond the school day, based on your professional need as a teacher, you are willing to commit to.

### Capable and Proficient Practitioners

1. Demonstrate an awareness of students' expectations of school and the degree to which those expectations are or are not being met.

2. Reflect on and explain why cultural responsiveness is a critical responsibility of all teachers and administrators.

3. Analyze, synthesize, and evaluate information and data gathered from the administration of learning style and interest inventories, and determine how the information will be used in teaching and learning.

4. Identify a professional development opportunity that increases your understanding of the expectations students have for school, learning, and teachers.

### Highly Skilled Practitioners

1. Examine a variety of strategies for building relationships with students, including learning about their cultures, employing culturally responsive pedagogy, and involving parents, families, and communities.

2. Access ongoing resources to support continued exploration of cultural responsiveness as an individual and as a school.

3. Share qualitative and relational metacognitive strategies with students that demonstrate effective cross-cultural communication and understanding.

4. Lead a professional development experience for your colleagues during a faculty meeting that specifically focuses on culturally responsive pedagogy.

### Expert

1. Write an action plan for fostering a culturally responsive learning environment in a sustained and meaningful way.

2. Access and assess resources that purport to support continued exploration of cultural responsiveness.

3. Share instructional strategies and processes with school and district colleagues on how to develop resiliency and perseverance in students via blogs, YouTube, or other social media outlets.

4. Add to the national discussion on serving Hispanic/Latino students by writing a position paper for a professional association or organization.

Professionally, effective teachers are skilled and have received training in implementing culturally responsive pedagogy. They also have expertise in differentiation of curriculum and instruction that continually challenges students, meets their needs, and guides them in working through the problems and frustrations encountered in the demonstration of learning. Personally, effective teachers need to be creative, lifelong learners who model the value and importance of intelligence, high standards, and achievements; who understand the impact of challenge, success, and failure; who encourage the pursuit of continuous intellectual development; and who recognize and respect the individual differences in students and their styles and methods of learning. Politically, effective teachers advocate for the need and value of developing and applying talent and potential to demonstrate learning and being able to communicate, collaborate, and cooperate with all stakeholders. Professionalization means that educators are culturally competent, always developing themselves, and caring. Through these characteristics, professional teachers ensure that equity, access, and opportunity are practiced within their classrooms in regard to their colleagues, their students, and themselves.

## Fluid Teaching

When instruction is developmental and flexible and infused with multicultural education, students are held accountable for their own learning and progress. This allows students in the same classroom and in the same school to work on a range of concepts and skills according to their own individual abilities, readiness levels, needs, and interests—the foundational ideal of fluid teaching. At the classroom level, Hispanic/Latino students have their own version of style, flair, and idiosyncratic nature in the form of readiness level, interest in learning, and resiliency. Mindsets are also different. Therefore, it makes perfect sense that instructional grouping practices embrace a fluidity and flexibility that allows students to be successful in a classroom that challenges them academically and intellectually without having to resort to a cookie-cutter, one-size-fits-all mentality. For example, keeping students identified as advanced or high-ability together makes sense. They need to be with others like themselves. Not placing them in the same classroom with students who fall far below in academic achievement or who have special needs also makes sense. The instructional range would simply be too great. Fluid and flexible instructional grouping should be the norm because it's student-centered and cost effective.

## Student-Centered

Student-centered education means personalized learning. Teachers take the time to assess their students for what they know, how they learn best, what areas need the most improvement, and what subjects they find the most interesting or relevant. This information should be gathered beginning on the first day and continuing throughout the school year with student self-reporting surveys and pretests for new sections.

Student surveys and pretesting allow us to avoid repetition. A significant cause of low student engagement is boredom. Scaffolding ensures high engagement by keeping the information students are asked to work with new to them. Scaffolding is an instructional strategy that builds on what students already know. When teachers and administrators include this as part of their daily practice, a culture of achievement is being created that serves as a solid foundation for building academic capacity. Building on what students already know saves valuable time, exposes students to a broader curricular experience, and allows teaching and learning to become personalized. Teachers recognize and value student input. In essence, when students' background knowledge in their interest areas is recognized and allowed to develop, content standards, benchmarks, and expectations are also honored.

Scaffolding is most effective when classes are organized into effective groups. Not all students will enter a subject area with the same background knowledge and interest. Cluster grouping allows the most similar students to be made into units that can be combined with other units to form cohesive classrooms. In programming for success, cluster grouping is a widely recommended and often used strategy for meeting the needs of students in the regular classroom.

One variation of the cluster group model is the Total School Cluster Grouping (TSCG) Model (Gentry & Mann, 2008), which takes into account the achievement levels of all students and places them in classrooms yearly in order to reduce the number of achievement levels in each classroom and to facilitate teachers' differentiation of curriculum and instruction for all students and thus increase student achievement. In this model, students are placed in one of five clusters (high-ability, above average, average, low average, low) where they will experience the most success. At the end of each quarter, or period of eight to ten weeks, students are reevaluated and allowed to move to other clusters based on their mastery of standards, objectives, and content. Hence, the TSCG Model is fluid and flexible and accommodates the needs of every student.

Adapted from the work of Gentry and Mann (2008), table 4.1 is an example of how the TSCG Model works.

Table 4.1: TSCG Model

| | Gifted/ High-Ability | Above Average | Average | Low Average | Low/Special Education |
|---|---|---|---|---|---|
| Class 1 | | | | | |
| Class 2 | | | | | |
| Class 3 | | | | | |
| Class 4 | | | | | |

*Rules of Engagement*

1. Gifted/high-ability students are never in the same class as low-achieving students. The gap is simply too great.

2. Gifted/high-ability students are never in the same group as above-average students. Consequently, above-average students now have an opportunity to shine in this new classroom configuration.

3. Each classroom has no more than three cluster groups, thus making instruction much more manageable.

4. Teachers are expected to reach a consensus about the labels assigned to students.

*Notes*

1. Use as much data as possible in making the assigned student cluster designation.

2. Clusters are meant to be fluid and flexible, allowing for student movement once standards, objectives, and skills have been mastered. Movement will occur, if needed, after each quarter.

3. The rule of thumb for fluid and flexible groups is that students may move across the same cluster or upward to the next highest cluster.

4.  Though it could be a consideration, the goal is not necessarily to have even classrooms in terms of numbers, but to do what is in the best interest of the students.

Table 4.2: Sample Classes Using the TSCG Model

|  | Gifted/ High Ability | Above Average | Average | Low-Average | Low/Special Education |
|---|---|---|---|---|---|
| Class 1 | 9 |  | 10 | 6 |  |
| Class 2 |  | 10 | 10 |  | 5 |
| Class 3 |  | 10 |  | 10 | 5 |
| Class 4 |  | 5 | 15 | 5 |  |

For Hispanic/Latino students, this particular grouping strategy recognizes their strengths and places them with others who are at similar achievement levels. A student may be placed in a high-ability cluster for reading and language arts, while being placed in an average cluster for math. And because instruction is now more manageable, each student has the potential to increase his or her academic achievement.

## Cost Effective

Fluid teaching, or instructional overhaul, is far more cost effective than the structural overhaul of reassigning students to different schools based on achievement. One strategy that has been implemented to combat challenges in equity and access is the creation of magnet schools. These efforts are intended to target and include Hispanic/Latino students and ELLs in theme-driven schools, such as performing arts, STEM, dual-language, and International Baccalaureate, for example. The United States Government Accountability Office (2016) reports that in school year 2000–2001, 3 percent of Hispanic students attended magnet schools; during the 2013–2014 school year, this enrollment increased to 5 percent. During this same period, the percentage of Hispanic students attending charter schools increased from 3 percent to 13 percent. Like magnet schools, many charter schools are theme-based, and they aim to provide access and opportunities the students would not purportedly receive in their local public school. The increase of Hispanic students attending magnet and charter schools translates to a significant decrease in their attendance at traditional neighborhood schools—from 94 percent in 2000–2001 down to 81 percent in 2013–2014.

Both magnet and charter schools attempt to fill a perceived void associated with traditional neighborhood schools by offering students something different in their programs, products, and services. However, because many of these schools are often located in the same community, they cannot escape the poverty that students bring with them. Furthermore, for students who do not live near these schools, the commuting time can sometimes be upward of an hour. The cost of bussing children back and forth across the county, as well as the cost of construction and staffing for new schools, is incredibly high. There will never be enough seats in charter or magnet schools to serve every Hispanic/Latino student who needs them, and there will never be enough money to keep creating more. By utilizing fluid teaching in the schools these students are already zoned for, we are utilizing available resources and revitalizing communities instead of passing the buck.

Fluid teaching also includes the validation of different types of learning. Perhaps one of the biggest challenges facing teachers and administrators is how to make what students are learning in the classroom meaningful beyond the classroom door. Not all (not most) students enjoy learning for the sake of gaining new knowledge. As long as we keep the "real world" and the "academic world" in separate spheres, students who do not identify as scholars will always feel they are guests in school, taking time and resources away from the select few "true students." This is especially true for Hispanic/Latino students, many of whom are the first in their family to even have the option of attending college. For these kids, applying new knowledge to audiences outside the school can help them engage their learning in a different way. In this context, students are given the opportunity to apply their knowledge, understanding, interests, strengths, and social networks to demonstrate what they know and can do in the real world. Offering academic-based experiences outside the traditional classroom also allows students to meet others who share a common interest. Connecting students to alumni provides meaningful exposure to careers, community service, and increased academic options and allows students a firsthand view of how they can make a difference. Two popular strategies for this crossover instruction are problem-based learning and project-based learning.

Problem-based learning occurs when students are challenged to learn about a subject by solving an open-ended problem found in material that triggers a response. The following steps to problem-based learning were retrieved from the Study Guides and Strategies website (www.studygs.net/pbl.htm), which includes more detail.

1. Explore the issues.

2. List what we know.

3. Develop and write out the problem statement in your own words.

4. List possible solutions.

5. List actions to be taken with a timeline.

6. List what we need to know.

7. Write up your solution with its supporting documentation, and submit it.

8. Present and defend your conclusions.

9. Review your performance.

10. Celebrate your work!

Project-based learning is also student-centered, and the inquiry-based instructional processes are targeted to empower students to acquire knowledge by actively exploring real-world challenges and problems that are relevant and meaningful. Presented earlier in the book, students serving as ambassadors for ensuring an accurate census count would be a good example of project-based learning. When I was a principal of an intermediate school serving grades 4–6, a group of students were concerned that there was not a big enough emphasis on or commitment from the school community toward recycling. I encouraged them to seek a faculty member who would be willing to sponsor a recycling club that would meet after school once a week. They did! In turn, I provided them with access to telephones, computers, and other resources they would need to further explore the reasons why recycling was not a priority and what could be done about it. Guest speakers were invited to the school and gave talks about the importance of recycling, the students visited a recycling plant, and they convinced the local waste management company to donate colored bins that would be strategically placed throughout the school community and for each member of the club to take home with the intention of teaching the importance of and practicing recycling. The students' success was everyone's success. This experience demonstrated the power of project-based learning that begins with a real-world challenge.

Personalized learning is a validation of the student's identity. Fluid teaching often creates a bond between teachers and students that pays dividends through increased academic achievement. The student is part of a relationship that is meaningful and healthy and expects accountability for learning. This bond is especially important to Hispanic/Latino students who aspire to attend college. Offering Hispanic/Latino students a continuum of choices that includes grouping by ability and/or potential empowers students to demonstrate their advanced knowledge and understanding. Acceleration and enrichment rather than remediation and compensation should be the norm, as should developing a focus on student strengths rather than on their deficits. To accommodate this caliber of student, teachers and administrators must model the application of advanced learning and understanding. And because many of our Hispanic/Latino students live in challenging, often dangerous communities, demonstrating support for their priorities through academic-based learning experiences outside the classroom can be an empowering and motivational strategy.

The fluid teacher must establish a balance between personalized learning, small-group guided lessons, and whole-class assignments consisting of multiple intelligences, varied learning styles and interests, authentic literacy experiences, and cooperative activities that measure key content standards, foster student engagement, and promote student choice, collaboration, and responsibility. To write it out is honestly much more difficult than to actually do it. Every teacher can utilize scaffolding and grouping in his or her classroom to provide personalized instruction for all the students, and principals who encourage fluid learning by schoolwide cluster grouping will see both better results for Hispanic/Latino students and a higher return on investment.

## Gifted or Remedial

One of the most disturbing and historical trends is our continued lack of commitment at all levels in identifying and serving Hispanic/Latino students who are gifted, advanced, or high-ability and in effectively identifying Hispanic/Latino children in need of special education. How and why we fail to properly serve these student populations is the subject of serious debate among stakeholder groups. This section outlines the competing explanations and offers strategies to better identify both gifted and special education students. If nothing else, this section should serve to make the reader aware of the uncountable nuances and confounding factors that influence how a child is sorted into different education tracks.

In the field of special education, there is an ongoing debate about the representation of black and Hispanic/Latino students identified as having special needs, outlined by the thirteen disability categories recognized by, and approved through, the Individuals with Disabilities Education Act (IDEA). Researchers, scholars, experts, and other stakeholder groups argue for both overrepresentation and underrepresentation. Education professors Paul L. Morgan from Pennsylvania State University and George Farkas from University of California, Irvine, as cited in Samuels (2016a) published a peer-reviewed analysis in 2015 stating that there is clear bias in the way students are identified for special education. But the bias went in an unexpected direction. By their calculations, black and Hispanic students are universally underrepresented compared to their white peers—rather than overrepresented—in a variety of categories, including emotional disturbance and specific learning disabilities. The researchers' paper situates itself squarely in the middle of debates on equity and racism. Morgan and Farkas suggest that teachers may be reluctant to refer students for special education for fear of being seen as racist and that they need training in culturally and linguistically sensitive evaluation methods.

Critics, on the other hand, argue that Morgan and Farkas are making sweeping and inaccurate conclusions based on data that don't reflect the actual population of students with disabilities, like Associate Professor Amanda L. Sullivan from the University of Minnesota, as cited in Samuels (2016a), and state that the number of students with disabilities in the data set used by Morgan and Farkas is very small and they are using those findings to suggest that underrepresentation is universal. Her own research has found that minorities are both underrepresented and overrepresented in some categories and that identification varies not only by disability category but by region of the United States.

The United States Department of Education's Office for Civil Rights has documented complaints regarding Hispanic/Latino students and special education reflecting both sides of this debate. In December of 2016, the Department of Education issued a final rule that could have a major impact on how districts spend their federal special education money. The department's regulation creates a standard approach that states must use in determining if their districts are overenrolling minority students in special education compared to their peers of other races. The new rule also requires states to use a standard approach to determine whether minority special education students are in segregated settings more than peers of other races. As reported by Samuels (2016b), Congress was clearly concerned about what it still saw as too many minorities in special education. So, it changed the law to say that if states found that some of their districts had "significant disproportionality," those districts would be required to spend 15 percent of their federal special education money on "coordinated, early intervention services." These dollars are not to be used for students already identified as having disabilities but on students who need additional academic and behavioral support to succeed in a general education environment. The money can be spent at any grade, but the Department of Education wants states to focus on kindergarten through third grades.

Students identified as special needs do impact local and state resources, especially in those states that have districts with high-poverty schools and where 75–100 percent of the students are also mostly Hispanic/Latino. Based on data from the Department of Education's Institute of Educational Sciences for years 2011–2012 and 2012–2013, Hispanic students are documented to be both underrepresented and overrepresented depending on the data set and category. For example, Hispanic/Latino students make up 25 percent of all public school students in K–12, but only 15 percent of them from three to twenty-one years of age were served under IDEA, Part B, by Race/Ethnicity for school year 2012–2013. Table 4.3 (page 86) documents the number and distribution of Hispanic children served by category and the number of Hispanic children served as a percent of total enrollment in special education for school years 2011–2012 and 2012–2013.

The data presented may lead one to summarize that in the category of specific learning disabilities, Hispanic students may be overrepresented, while they appear to be slightly underrepresented in the category of speech and language impairment, autism, and emotional disturbance. Friend and Bursuck (2015) add that many reasons have been proposed to explain issues of disproportionate representation, including the influence of poverty and the impact of cultural and linguistic differences between students and their teachers. Needless to say, how one interprets the data will influence what side of the disproportionality debate they side with. This decision may be further influenced when Spanish-speaking ELLs are factored into the discussion. Is an ELL demonstrating a need for a possible special education placement, or is he or her simply experiencing normal second language acquisition stages of development?

The decision to refer an ELL of Hispanic descent for possible special education placement must include a comprehensive evaluation of what that student knows and

Table 4.3: Hispanic Children Three to Twenty-One Years Old Served Under Individuals with Disabilities Education Act, Part B, and Type of Disability, 2011–2012 and 2012–2013

| | 2011–2012 | | 2012–2013 | |
| --- | --- | --- | --- | --- |
| | Percentage of Distribution of Hispanic Children Served | Number of Hispanic Children Served as a Percent of Total Enrollment | Percentage of Distribution of Hispanic Children Served | Number of Hispanic Children Served as a Percent of Total Enrollment |
| Autism | 5.7 | 0.7 | 6.5 | 0.8 |
| Deaf-Blindness | # Rounds to 0 | # Rounds to 0 | # Rounds to 0 | # Rounds to 0 |
| Developmental Delay | 5.0 | 0.6 | 4.9 | 0.6 |
| Emotional Disturbance | 3.8 | 0.4 | 3.7 | 0.4 |
| Hearing Impairment | 1.6 | 0.2 | 1.5 | 0.2 |
| Intellectual Disability | 6.3 | 0.7 | 6.4 | 0.7 |
| Multiple Disabilities | 1.7 | 0.2 | 1.6 | 0.2 |
| Orthopedic Impairment | 1.2 | 0.1 | 1.1 | 0.1 |
| Other Health Impairments | 7.6 | 0.9 | 8.1 | 0.9 |
| Specific Learning Disability | 43.6 | 5.0 | 43.1 | 5.0 |
| Speech/Language Impairment | 22.7 | 2.6 | 22.3 | 2.6 |
| Traumatic Brain Injury | 0.3 | # Rounds to 0 | 0.3 | # Rounds to 0 |
| Visual Impairment | 0.5 | 0.1 | 0.4 | 0.1 |
| **TOTALS** | **100.0** | **11.6** | **100.0** | **11.7** |

is able to do. Considerations include areas to be assessed, sources for obtaining assessment data, and who gathers the information. This collection of evidence at the point of service will help a school's or district's child study team determine if a placement is warranted. There is common agreement in the field that what is to be assessed must be discussed and agreed to by parents in order to comply with federal procedural safeguards. The sources for obtaining assessment data must also be clearly spelled out and typically include both quantitative and qualitative information about a student. Equally important, if not more so, is identifying who will gather the information. Response to intervention (RTI) and the multi-tiered system of support (MTSS) may also be part of the process.

## Areas to Be Assessed

- Cognitive ability
  - Verbal
  - Nonverbal
- Academic achievement
  - Reading
  - Writing
  - Math
- Language
  - Phonology
  - Morphology
  - Syntax
- Lexicon
- Semantics
- Current classroom performance
  - Reading
  - Writing
  - Math
- Learning characteristics
- Motivation
- Social adaptation
  - Formal and informal

## Sources for Obtaining Assessment Data

- Tests of cognitive ability/intelligence (English and/or Spanish)
- Tests of academic achievement (English and/or Spanish)
- Language proficiency assessments (English and Spanish)
- Current/past report cards
- Progress reports
- Performance-based products/projects
- Characteristics checklist
- Writing sample
- Cumulative files
- Portfolio
- Interviews/conferences

## Who Gathers the Information?

- Psychologist
  - Monolingual
  - Bilingual
- Diagnostician/evaluator
  - Monolingual
  - Bilingual
- Parent(s)/guardian
- Student
- Regular classroom teacher
- ESL/bilingual teacher
- Building administrators
- Local education agency (LEA) representative
- Other adults who can support/refute referral
  - From community
  - Therapist
  - Counselor
  - Advocate

One of the most important decisions to be made is whether to conduct the assessments in English or Spanish. Ideally, a bilingual school psychologist, diagnostician, and other bilingual district special education personnel should be considered for their ability to use both languages to elicit the most valid and reliable information from the student. Furthermore, these processes should become part of a school's and district's nonnegotiables and tied to policies, practices, and procedures.

## Policies

- The school district offers a continuum of special education services based on the principle of least restrictive environment (found in IDEA).
- Parents are informed and included in program planning and implementation (found in IDEA).
- Information about special education is provided to parents in their heritage language (found in IDEA).
- Teachers and administrators who work with special needs students who are culturally and linguistically diverse receive training in cultural competency.
- ELLs with special needs may also be considered for gifted education or other advanced academic programs.
- Identification, assessment, and evaluation, as well as program options, are clearly stated (found in IDEA).
- The special education program is evaluated yearly, particularly in the area of diversity.

## Procedures

- Selected assessment protocols and related procedures will include both nonverbal quantitative measures and qualitative information collected from parents, teachers, and others.

- ELLs can receive both special education services (including gifted education), as well as ESL, bilingual, or dual-language services.

- There is a district-level special education advisory board that represents the diversity of the school community.

- The school district collects data on the eligibility patterns of its special education programs.

- Special education data are analyzed by socioeconomic status, race, ethnicity, and by the numbers of ELLs identified and served.

## Practices

- ESL and/or bilingual teachers, in addition to regular education teachers, are included in the assessment process.

- There is a climate of high expectations, and all students are expected to achieve.

- Individualized education plans (IEPs) include cultural connections, language goals, and other objectives to meet their unique social and emotional needs.

- RTI is a routine practice used in the district, school, and classroom.

As a former bilingual special education teacher and an administrator in special education for both school and district levels, I trademarked the ELL/SPED (English language learner / Special education) Screening Instrument to assist regular, bilingual, ESL, and special education teachers and administrators in determining whether an ELL is experiencing normal second language acquisition processing or, indeed, has a learning problem. Rooted in research, evidence, and practice, the instrument requires educators who have direct instructional contact with the student to answer yes or no to sixteen primary questions and four additional qualifying questions for data-gathering purposes (figure 4.1, page 90). The goal is for a team of educators to make an informed decision that truly reflects the ability of any given ELL using multiple evidence-based data points documented by the yes or no questions.

1. Twelve or more yes responses (75 percent) indicate that the challenge the student is experiencing is normal/developmental second language acquisition processing and should improve with time and practice.

2. Twelve or more no responses (75 percent) indicate that the student may have a learning disability and should be referred to a school's child study team for further review.

3. If the student does not achieve 75 percent in either area, it is quite possible that he or she is developing/achieving at his or her "potential" level. Multiple evidence sources should support a student's potential level.

---

**Is It a Learning Disability or Normal Second Language Acquisition Processing?**

A Checklist to Determine the Difference

Student Name: _____ District ID # _____ School _____ Date _____

Teacher Completing Checklist: _____ Grade Level _____ Birthday _____ Age ____

| | Criteria | Yes | No | Evidence Source (to support choice) |
|---|---|---|---|---|
| 1 | Is the student able to demonstrate mastery of grade-level language skills? | | | |
| 2 | Are attempts to reteach successful? | | | |
| 3 | Is the student able to self-correct language skills and/or ability (verb tenses, grammar)? | | | |
| 4 | Do formal and informal assessment measures document progress in language learning? | | | |
| 5 | Do classroom assignments show progress with expressive language? | | | |
| 6 | Is the student making satisfactory progress mastering English language development (ELP) standards in listening, speaking, reading, and writing (L/S/R/W)? | | | |
| 7 | Do error corrections after modeling lead to improved use of the English language? | | | |
| 8 | Does the student have a vocabulary appropriate for his/her age and grade level? | | | |
| 9 | Is the student able to acquire academic language through content-based lessons? | | | |
| 10 | Are language and/or learning problems noted in his/her primary language? | | | |
| 11 | Does the student have difficulty with listening/receptive language skills (following directions, retaining instruction)? | | | |
| 12 | Is the student able to retain basic academic skills? | | | |

| | Criteria | Yes | No | Evidence Source (to support choice) |
|---|---|---|---|---|
| 13 | Is the student able to generalize learned skills in other contexts or environments? | | | |
| 14 | Is response to intervention (RTI) successful? | | | |
| 15 | Are language or learning difficulties also noted by other adults who have contact with the student? | | | |
| 16 | Does the student make progress participating in tutoring and/or summer school program? | | | |
| Additional Qualifying Questions for Data Gathering and Discussion | | | | |
| | **Criteria** | **Yes** | **No** | **Evidence Source** (to support choice) |
| 17 | Do parents note lack of progress in language development and academic achievement? | | | |
| 18 | Does the student acknowledge difficulty in language development and/or academic achievement? | | | |
| 19 | Is the student stuck at a particular English proficiency level despite repeated assessments? | | | |
| 20 | Does the student become frustrated with completing routine classroom assignments? | | | |

**Figure 4.1: ELL/SPED (English Language Learner/Special Education) Screening Instrument.**

The ELL/SPED Screening Instrument has assisted schools across the country as an advocacy and equity tool, helping them make valid and reliable decisions on behalf of students and their parents.

The other half of the special education coin is gifted and talented education. Since the 1970s, Hispanic/Latino students have been underrepresented in advanced academic programs like gifted education (Castellano & Dias, 2002; Castellano, 2003, 2011; Plucker et al., 2015). In their Jack Kent Cooke Foundation document titled *Equal Talents, Unequal Opportunities: A Report Card on State Support for Academically Talented Low-Income Students*, Plucker et al. (2015) write that year after year, in every state and community in our nation, students from low-income families are less likely than other students to reach advanced levels of academic performance, even when demonstrating the potential to do so. These income-based "excellence gaps" appear in elementary school and continue through high school. It is a story of demography predetermining destiny, with bright low-income students becoming a persistent talent underclass.

The Government Accountability Office (2016) provides statistical data that seemingly supports the conclusions of the Jack Kent Cooke Foundation. That is, when looking at school type (traditional, charter, magnet), Hispanic students who attend high-poverty schools are underrepresented in each one. Ford (2014) adds that an examination of 2009 and 2011 data from the Office for Civil Rights Data Collection revealed that underrepresentation exists in all states and in the majority of school districts. More recently, it reported that Hispanic students comprise 25 percent of students in public schools but only 16 percent of students in gifted education, which equates to 36 percent underrepresentation. Although it is essential for teachers and administrators to know the percentage of underrepresentation for Hispanic/Latino students, no underrepresentation formula suffices for determining what is unacceptable, unreasonable, or illegal/discriminatory underrepresentation, nor is the formula specific enough to set goals for improving representation. As presented by Ford (2014), calculating the equity index for Hispanics is a two-step process.

- Step 1:
  - Composition / percentage of Hispanic students in general education: C = 25 percent
  - Equity threshold: T = 20 percent
  - This is abbreviated to C − T = A, or 25 − 20 = 5.0

- Step 2:
  - Composition / percentage of Hispanic students in general education: C = 25 percent
  - Subtract A, or 5.0
  - The full formula is abbreviated as C − A = equity index (25 − 5 = 20); equity index is 20 percent.

For Hispanic/Latino students nationally, the equity index is approximately 20 percent for 2013. Given that they represent almost 16 percent of gifted education rather than the minimal 20 percent when viewed through an equity perspective, Hispanic/Latino students are also underrepresented beyond statistical probability. Though rudimentary in its presentation, Ford's equity index results are consistent with all other data sets that conclude that Hispanics/Latinos are an underrepresented group in gifted education. This analysis of equity data can also serve as a catalyst for initiating dialogue and changing how we identify, assess, and serve Hispanic/Latino students, not only in gifted education, but in all advanced academic programs that a district offers.

Why do educators consistently fail to recommend Hispanic/Latino students for gifted education? Part of the answer lies in the previous chapters of this book. For Hispanic/Latino students living here undocumented, in poverty, and facing conflicting notions of identity, there are often limits on equity, access, and opportunity. Educators who fail to involve family in the child's learning, care for the whole child, and incorporate Hispanic/Latino culture in their classrooms are failing to take into account the sheer amount of perseverance a gifted Hispanic/Latino student must have to be recognized.

The basic premise of the perseverance model (figure 4.2, page 94) is that the further away from mainstream America poor Hispanic/Latino students are, the more resiliency and perseverance they need to demonstrate in order to overcome the challenges of gaining access to gifted education programs. It represents both individual and institutional variables that impact issues of equity and access and can be seen as a validation of the need to review and include a cross section of information and data when identifying Hispanics/Latinos for gifted education. The areas that comprise the perseverance model include:

- **Identification**—Identification typically begins at the classroom level and includes an analysis of how the student demonstrates the need for advanced academic services. Whether teachers have been trained to identify gifted behavior in Hispanic/Latino students and ELLs influences the rate of nominations and referrals.

- **Assessment and Evaluation**—Determining what is in the best interest of the students should be the overriding consideration. Discussions about best practices in assessing and evaluating Hispanic/Latino students with IQ and achievement tests must be part of the dialogue among child study team members.

- **Socialized Environment**—Often overlooked in the identification process, the influence of the peer group and how the individual navigates through relationships with it and the community in which he or she lives is often reflective of his or her resilient nature. What kind of leadership skills is he or she demonstrating?

- **Dynamics of the Home**—Multiple variables describing the dynamics of the home offer further evidence of gifted behavior. Often, the child also demonstrates gifted behavior associated with his or her particular ethnicity.

- **Dynamics of the School**—The dynamics of the school can work either in favor of or against Hispanic/Latino students trying to gain access to its gifted education program. Whether teachers have been trained to identify gifted behavior in historically underserved students influences the rate of nominations and referrals.

- **Language Patterns**—In the perseverance model, identifying the language patterns of the student is crucial. This information can dictate in what language to administer individual assessments. It is also important to know if the student can manipulate his or her language patterns in different environments and for different audiences (pragmatics of language).

- **Acculturation**—The dynamics of the home and related language patterns often signify the acculturation level of the student. This is important information that may influence in what language to test and what type of

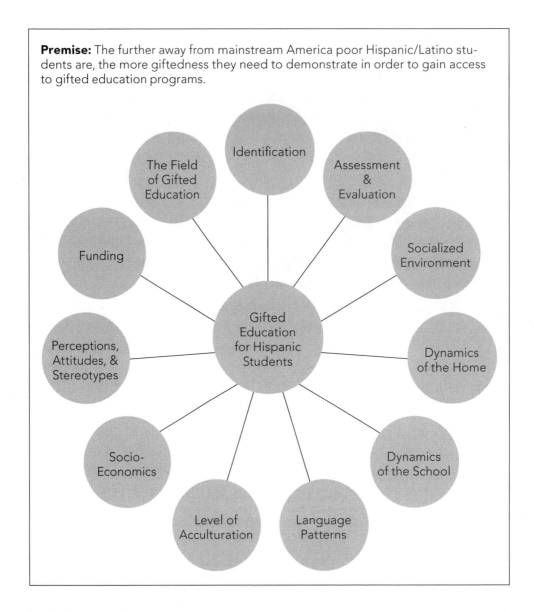

**Premise:** The further away from mainstream America poor Hispanic/Latino students are, the more giftedness they need to demonstrate in order to gain access to gifted education programs.

**Figure 4.2: The perseverance model: Gifted education for Hispanic/Latino students.**

IQ test to use. The acculturation of the father may dictate the participation in a gifted program of Hispanic/Latino girls.

- **Socioeconomics**—Poverty typically restricts a child's experiences and knowledge levels. Consequently, it confounds a process designed to identify and select our best, brightest, and most able students. Middle- and upper-class Hispanic/Latino students may have a better chance of accessing gifted education programs in their schools.

- **Perceptions, Attitudes, and Stereotypes**—There are a myriad of reasons why Hispanic/Latino and other students continue to be underrepresented in gifted education. The perceptions, attitudes, and stereotypes of program gatekeepers are often the result of ignorance and misinformation and prevent many of our most gifted Hispanic/Latino students from accessing the programs that are their right.

- **Funding**—Many schools and districts fail to receive the necessary funding to even implement a program that offers a continuum of services based on need. As a result, Hispanic/Latino students who may be eligible are shut out of services from the very beginning. With a lack of funding comes a lack of training, resources, and personnel in identifying and serving gifted Hispanic/Latino students.

- **The Field of Gifted Education**—As long as the status quo is allowed to perpetuate itself, we will always have large groups of students shut out of gifted education programming. We are at a point in the history of gifted education in the United States where more proactive and inclusive decisions would benefit a wider population of students.

Peters and Engerrand (2016) report that a major barrier to greater equity in the identification of students for gifted and talented programs is that, on average, students from Hispanic/Latino and low-income backgrounds, among others, receive lower observed scores on tests of academic achievement and ability than do their Caucasian, Asian, and higher-income peers. ELLs also have lower observed scores, though differences in ability are confounded to some extent by the specific language demands of the test. In the past, the field of gifted education has approached these observed score differences, and the underrepresentation that is the result, using two perceived solutions: use different tests and use tests differently (Peters & Engerrand, 2016).

### Use Different Tests

Under the "use different tests" perspective, culture-neutral or bias-free tests and assessment methods are recommended for identification. Frequently mentioned is the use of a nonverbal test of cognitive ability or achievement protocols that include a nonverbal subtest of some sort. Peters and Engerrand (2016) go on to add that even if culture-neutral tests exist, they are not likely to align well with the most common types of gifted programming—a problem of content validity—where Hispanic/Latino and other underrepresented groups gain access through these nonverbal, culture-neutral measures but where programs are verbally rich and language intensive. What matters is that the measure or measures used for identification are closely aligned to the intervention (gifted education) for which the student is identified. This criteria is the single most important characteristic of a strong, equitable identification system.

*Use Tests Differently*

In this perspective, a school district uses instruments already in place but in a different way—specifically by using different norm samples. In using local norms, a school focuses on the question of which students are the most advanced and therefore most likely underchallenged and in need of additional services, compared to other students in the same school or district. Local norms, especially at the building level, make the most sense for gifted identification because they identify the students who would most likely benefit from additional advanced intervention—following the logic that those students who are farthest from typical in a given school are the most likely to be underchallenged. Such decisions should also be made locally because it is locally that a child is or is not appropriately challenged, and it will be locally within a particular school that any intervention will be provided.

What do we mean by *intervention*? If a school doesn't have a dedicated gifted teaching staff and classrooms, as most lower-income schools don't, there are still means by which to provide challenging and relevant instruction for highly motivated students. For Hispanic/Latino students in these schools, acceleration can be one of the most effective strategies. Acceleration as a service delivery may include grade-skipping, subject-skipping, and part-time acceleration (entering a higher grade for part of the day) to receive instruction in one or more subjects. Acceleration as a curricular model involves speeding up the pace at which material is presented, expected to be mastered, or both. For those students who are fluent in reading, writing, and speaking Spanish and are enrolled in a bilingual program or in a foreign language program at the secondary level, opportunities for acceleration also exist.

## Programming for Success: Project ExCEL

The purpose of Project ExCEL is to scale-up a proven program to provide high-ability, low-income (HA-LI) middle-school-aged gifted students with experiences cultivating exceptional learning (ExCEL). The objectives of Project ExCEL are to: (1) increase identification of HA-LI middle school students, (2) improve achievement in English language arts (ELA), and (3) build students' motivation for learning and sense of academic self-efficacy and provide challenging curricular experiences. Additionally, Project ExCEL strives to develop teachers' understanding of the characteristics of gifted students and knowledge of problem-based learning curricula and instruction.

The Project ExCEL model takes place in two sequences, Find and Serve. During the first sequence, Find, a universal screening takes place in seventh-grade ELA general education classes. Teachers implement two problem-based learning units, based on the model adapted for K–12 education from medical school as described by Stepien and Pyke (1997). Teachers select potentially gifted students based on their observations of students' performance during these units and based on the students' results on formative and summative assessments. While Project ExCEL uses an experimental design, one of the strengths of the model is that all of the selected students are scheduled for eighth-grade advanced ELA classes, with the treatment group receiving the intervention of problem-based learning. The model continues in eighth grade with the second sequence of the project, Serve, and the implementation of the intervention of problem-based learning in the treatment classes.

To date, preliminary results from Project ExCEL have provided some encouraging evidence. Initial findings indicate that problem-based learning instruction is effective in increasing student achievement for all students but is particularly effective for ELLs. During the first year of Project ExCEL, the achievement gap between ELLs and non-ELLs on problem-based learning content tests was closed, and the gap narrowed significantly in the second year. In addition, achievement gaps on standardized end-of-year assessments narrowed significantly. These results were significant for all ELLs and specifically for Hispanic/Latino ELLs (Horak, Holincheck, Webb, & Nagy, 2017).

Project ExCEL identified high-ability, low-income students who are more representative of the school population than those found using traditional identification methods, meeting Ford's (2014) equity index for identification of low-income and Hispanic students. Project ExCEL has made significant gains in identifying HA-LI ELLs when compared with traditional identification methods (Horak, Holincheck, Webb, & Nagy, 2017).

Teachers frequently comment on their experience with the influence problem-based learning instruction has on ELLs. For example:

> It was a really interesting dynamic because if you put [ELLs] in a situation where there is enough structure, but a challenge, they will rise to it. But then also it was really interesting to see that we have made our classroom a safe place for them to be able to take chances. (Teacher, second year with Project ExCEL)

When ELLs speak to their experience in a problem-based learning classroom, the theme of the importance of independent inquiry emerges: "I think it was a lot more cooperative and a lot more student-based. The teacher didn't really interfere so we used our minds to get it. I really liked that" (eighth-grade student, Project ExCEL).

Outcomes from Project ExCEL suggest problem-based learning has a positive impact on achievement and functions as an alternative pathway to increase opportunities for identification for advanced classes for ELLs, specifically HA-LI Hispanic/Latino students. This alternative pathway for identification may work in conjunction with traditional identification processes to provide not just a multiple-criteria approach but rather a multiple-criteria, multiple-pathways approach that broadens the integrity of traditional approaches and reflects a growing trend of practices for recruitment and retention in other areas (National Science Board, 2010).

## Programming for Success: Individual Learning Plans

The individual learning plan (ILP) is a personalized document that students develop with their teacher and parents to chart their progress toward their academic goals during each school year. The plan also determines what resources and tools they need to be successful. Because many of our Hispanic/Latino students are enrolled in bilingual programs and take Spanish in middle school or high school, developing a plan in Spanish is acceptable. Through the ILP, the student should be challenged, working in his or her zone of proximal development, meaning that achieving the goals of the learning plan should not necessarily be easy where little effort is required. Nor should the plan be so complex that completing it would result in failure or disappointment. The ILP should be somewhere in between. The student will be provided the guidance and motivation to complete the actions required to be successful. The Internet has an abundance of sample templates that can be used, or they can be developed at the local level by a team of educators.

Involving parents and other stakeholder groups in identifying Hispanic/Latino students for special or gifted education improves the efficacy of these assignments. Accounting for how much a student has had to overcome just to get to the classroom and how being an ELL might affect his or her performance is also critical. With the rubrics provided, schools should be better able to serve their neediest and highest-achieving students more effectively.

## Raise the Floor and Ceiling

"For better or worse, policies mirror priorities and actions speak louder than words." In 2012, Olszewski-Kubilius and Clarenbach used these words to emphasize that national and many state, district, and school policies and practices do not reflect a commitment to talent development of low-income gifted students. As a nation, we are concerned with the achievement of low-income and minority students but have not focused on advancing more of those students to exceptional levels of performance and achievement. To move forward, we must ask ourselves whether aiming for minimal performance levels for all students is an acceptable singular goal for the nation and whether achieving minimal levels requires that we abandon support for a goal of more students reaching advanced levels of achievement. The answer to this question must be an emphatic NO.

One criticism often leveraged against the No Child Left Behind legislation was its emphasis on proficiency, of meeting the lowest common denominator. Consequently, the vast majority of efforts by educators across the country was a laser-like focus on bringing up the bottom, their lowest-achieving students, to the exclusion of all other student needs. This course of action shifted both human and financial resources to only one segment of the complex populations in our schools. For Title I schoolwide projects, this allocation created inequities and lack of access and opportunity for students who were not among the lowest achieving by not providing the same level of resources.

Today, there is a call to action to get school-based and district-based administrators to realize that to actualize the talent of all students, the raising of the floor and ceiling must occur simultaneously. In schools where this is already beginning, we can see some of the most incredible stories of success.

The website of Okeeheelee Middle School, located in Greenacres, Florida, documents that in May of 2017, fourteen students in the International Spanish Academy (ISA) at Okeeheelee Middle School and the School District of Palm Beach County, Florida, were given the opportunity to take the Advanced Placement (AP) exam in Spanish Language and Culture, and all fourteen of the eighth graders passed. Of the fourteen students, one scored a 3, eight scored a 4, and five scored a 5 on the college-level exam that allows students to earn college credit or receive advanced placement in college courses. The students were able to pass the test with less than a semester of AP-focused preparation. With the success of the program, Okeeheelee Middle School is offering three sections of AP Spanish Language and Culture to more than sixty students during the 2017–2018 school year.

Raising the floor and ceiling means that we raise our expectations of the least we expect of our students and the most we ask of them. Part of this is recognizing that students on the high end of a school's achievement continuum also require specialized instruction through specialized programs, products, and services, not just those at the lowest end. The other part is analyzing why we expect some results from certain student populations and not others. Raising the floor and ceiling must also apply to our expectations for ourselves as educators. It isn't enough for us to identify and distance ourselves from the worst; as educators, we need to raise the ceiling on what we consider the best. We can achieve this with reflection, recognition, and application.

## Reflection

Part of our collective journey to leveling the playing field involves engaging ourselves in a process of self-reflection, self-assessment, and understanding how we perceive others who are different from ourselves. This self-examination will help us gain a clearer understanding of our own experiences, boundaries, and challenges. Any educator who has contact with Hispanic/Latino students will benefit from this self-review process. As a result of the self-assessment and evaluation of their own cultural identity, educators begin to understand how they influence teaching and learning. Reflection informs change, and it is this shift in mindset that promotes actions and behaviors consistent with advocacy, hope, and inspiration.

How national discussions on socioeconomic inequities trickle down to the state and local levels is often determined by the perceptions and expectations held by school board members, administrators, and teachers. Their values, beliefs, and understandings are often informed by personal interactions and life experiences with a particular group of people. How these views are formed plays a role in their behaviors, actions taken, and their perceptions, in this case, about the achievement capability of Hispanic/Latino students. Gender, racial, and cultural differences between teachers and students may also help us better understand why the problem persists.

*The problem* and other such euphemistic allusions are easier to discuss than the word *racism*. We become defensive and resistant to dialogue under the threat of being labeled a racist, and for good reason; a teacher who gains such a reputation loses the respect of the students and his or her peers, and often loses his or her job. As a result, we need to be careful in how we discuss racism within our schools, and it *is* within our schools. Baylor (2016) found that according to an analysis of teacher attitudes, educators believed that Hispanic students were 42 percent less likely to earn a college diploma than their white classmates. Though this statistic may be difficult to fathom, it clearly reveals how some teachers have difficulty in connecting and establishing meaningful relationships with their Hispanic/Latino students. Generalizations, stereotypes, bias, racism—are they inherent, or are they learned behavior? What can be done to facilitate a growth mindset through which Hispanic/Latino students are seen as having talent and potential and teachers and administrators embrace the cultural capital of their students and model effective cross-cultural communication and understanding?

As documented by Brophy (1983) and O'Conner and DeLuca-Fernandez (2006), abrupt changes in the student population can lead to cultural mismatches and misunderstandings. When teachers have negative perceptions of students, it can adversely impact student behavior and lead to measurable declines in achievement. Teachers unfamiliar with low-income or minority students are likely to view them as not ready for school or unprepared for grade-level work. Cultural differences can easily be mistaken as expressions of learning or emotional disability. This deficit model sets generations of Hispanic/Latino students far behind the starting line before the race even begins. Schools that are mindful of diversity, especially the intra-ethnic diversity found among Hispanic/Latino parents and families, must remember that they also represent a broad range of family structures reflective of the greater United States:

+ Married parents

+ An LGBT parent

+ Blended families

+ Same-sex parents

+ Stay-at-home moms, stay-at-home dads

+ Single-parent families

+ Non-English-speaking, limited-English-speaking parents/families

- Parents and families outside the school boundaries; children are bussed

- Families in temporary shelters, homeless

- Biracial, bicultural families

- Undocumented, immigrant parents and families

- Uneducated parents

- Highly educated parents

- Parents and families living in poverty

- An incarcerated parent

You will never have a classroom of students who reflect exactly your heritage, up-bringing, values, and beliefs; each home is unique. If we engaged only with students who were identical to us, we would never teach anybody. Teachers and administrators who know how to forge social-emotional connections with their students from all backgrounds are in a position to change the world. There is no other profession that not only allows, but actively *requires*, its employees to be a significant influence on the next generation. It is a great gift and a great responsibility. Here is how to engage in honest self-reflection practices to ensure internal bias does not impede your ability to shape the future:

1. As a building principal, district office leader, and university professor, I have often asked my colleagues and students to reflect on and then rate their level of perceived effectiveness in engaging in cross-cultural communication and understanding and their ability to accept diversity, using a scale of one to ten, with one being "I am not effective" to ten being "I am very effective." Afterward, we have a discussion on the prompt, and individuals are free to share their score and tell why they scored themselves the way they did. I end the discussion with the rhetorical question, "What is the evidence that supports your score?" This requires additional personal reflection.

2. With my preservice teacher education candidates, I routinely engage them in reflection techniques that are designed to make them think about how they will foster relationships with their students. A prompt that serves as an example is: "How will you create an inclusive classroom that honors the unique needs of each student?" This open-ended, inquiry-based question helps prepare them for their first teaching position. During class, I meet with them in small groups to further engage with the question.

3. As a school principal, I informally meet with first- and second-year teachers on a monthly basis to see how they are doing and to answer any questions they may have. One of my opening questions may be: "How

are you different from, yet similar to, the students you are teaching?" I intentionally leave the room for about five to ten minutes to give them time to reflect on the question. I ask them not to write anything but to simply think about the prompt. Upon my return, I ask a related question: "How will you use this information in your teaching and learning?"

4. As a professional development trainer, keynote speaker, consultant, and scholar, I often ask the audience I address to reflect on and then identify a successful and a not-so-successful experience in meeting the social and emotional needs of their racially, culturally, and linguistically diverse students. Next, I ask them to think about both experiences and then to identify the causes for why one experience was successful and the other not so successful. To close the process, I encourage them to share their thoughts with a colleague they feel comfortable with and who will be nonjudgmental (which requires additional reflection).

5. In working with and training other school administrators and district leaders, I often close our first hour together by asking them the following question: "Do you believe a school's or district's advanced academic programs should reflect the demographics it serves? Why?" In my experience, this question has left some of our colleagues feeling a bit uncomfortable as shown in their facial expressions and body language. There is no discussion that follows, but there is an understanding that they will continue to reflect on how their behaviors have a direct effect on this question and on the students they serve.

## Recognition

Internal bias exists in all of us. How does it manifest in our schools? Once you know what to look for, it is disturbing how easy it can be found. In her 2016 report to the president of the United States and the secretary of education titled *Securing Equal Education Opportunity*, then assistant secretary for civil rights Catherine E. Lhamon writes that in schools throughout our nation, students continue to lack access to a quality education or face barriers in the form of discrimination, harassment, violence, or discipline. Here are a few of the documented cases and examples found in the 2016 Securing Equal Educational Opportunity Report by the United States Department of Education's Office for Civil Rights.

- **College and Career Readiness:** Black and Latino students have less access to high-level math and science courses. Student enrollment in AP courses is unequal.

  - Thirty-three percent of high schools with high black and Latino student enrollment (75–100 percent) offer calculus, compared to 56 percent of high schools with low black and Latino student enrollment (0–25 percent).

> ‣ Forty-eight percent of high schools with high black and Latino student enrollment offer physics, compared to 67 percent of high schools with low black and Latino student enrollment.

> ‣ Black and Latino students represent 38 percent of students in schools that offer AP courses but 29 percent of students enrolled in at least one AP course.

> ‣ ELLs represent 5 percent of students in schools that offer AP courses but 2 percent of students enrolled in at least one AP course.

- **Chronic Student Absenteeism:** Nationwide, more than 6.8 million students—or 14 percent of all students—are chronically absent (absent fifteen or more days during the school year).

> ‣ Twenty-one percent of Latino students are chronically absent from high school.

> ‣ Twenty-one percent of all ELLs are chronically absent.

- **Teacher and Staffing Equity:** Latino students, among other groups, are more likely to attend schools with higher concentrations of inexperienced teachers.

> ‣ Six percent of Latino students attend schools where more than 20 percent of teachers are in their first year of teaching, compared to 3 percent of white students and 3 percent of Asian students.

Title VI of the Civil Rights Act of 1964 prohibits discrimination on the basis of race, color, or national origin in programs and activities operated by recipients of federal funds. It states: "No person in the United States shall, on the ground of race, color, or national origin, be excluded from participation in, be denied the benefits of, or be subjected to discrimination under any program or activity receiving federal financial assistance." In the education arena, Title VI's protections apply to all public elementary and secondary schools and colleges and universities—public or private— that receive federal financial assistance. Its protections extend to all aspects of these institutions' programs and activities.

During FY 2016, the Office for Civil Rights received 2,439 complaints raising Title VI issues. Of these complaints:

- 976 referenced different treatment, exclusion, or denial of benefits

- 99 referenced ELLs

- 7 referenced minorities in special education

- 528 referenced racial harassment
- 9 referenced resource equity and comparability

### The Complaint against Albuquerque Public Schools

In March of 2016, the Office for Civil Rights resolved a complaint alleging that Albuquerque Public Schools discriminated on the basis of national origin by failing to respond adequately to the complainant's claims of harassment of students and parents by school teachers. Specifically, the complainant alleged that several staff members belittled students and parents of Latino descent in their tone and speech. During the course of the investigation, the office found that the district did not investigate the allegations about the harassment of Spanish-speaking students and parents. Additionally, it found that the district discriminated on the basis of national origin by failing to provide the school's ELLs with language development services taught by teachers with the appropriate state-required education endorsements. In its resolution agreement with the Office for Civil Rights, the district agreed to revise its policies and procedures and provide staff training on how to respond to allegations of harassment. Moreover, the district agreed to designate an administrator or consultant to review all complaints of national origin and/or racial harassment and identify if actions are needed to redress the effects of a hostile environment.

### The Complaint against Jefferson Parish Public Schools (Louisiana)

In October of 2015, the Office for Civil Rights entered into a resolution agreement with Jefferson Parish Public Schools after two separate complainants alleged discrimination against ELLs based on their national origin by failing to provide them with equal educational opportunities. The office investigated whether the district failed to provide equal educational opportunities to national-origin-minority ELLs by failing to provide appropriate staffing and staff development in its alternative language program and improperly placing and exiting ELLs, a violation of Title VI. When reviewing the district's ESL and paraprofessional staff at its schools, the office identified concerns regarding inconsistent or high student-to-teacher ratios for ELLs and a lack of information to conclude whether or not the district designated paraprofessionals to service ELLs. Prior to the conclusion of the investigation, the district entered into a resolution agreement committing the district to assessing whether it has sufficient qualified teachers and staff support to run its alternative language program, hiring additional certified alternative language program teachers if necessary, improving its evaluation of ESL teachers, providing training for teachers and teachers' aides on ESL instructional methodologies, revising its policies and monitoring student progress to ensure proper identification for and exiting from alternative language instruction, and reporting to the Office for Civil Rights on progress made in these areas.

## Application

Data collection, monitoring, and appraisal are the first steps toward the application of a school's self-reflection and recognition of problem areas. Here are six questions schools should be asking about their data:

1. Does the district collect data on the eligibility patterns of its gifted education program?

2. Is the data analyzed by socioeconomic status, race, ethnicity, poverty, and languages spoken?

3. Have programs and policies been put in place as a result of such data analysis?

4. Does the district work with stakeholder groups in interpreting this data?

5. Is there a policy that calls for a yearly program evaluation, particularly in the area of diversity?

6. What are the perceived barriers preventing Hispanic/Latino students from gaining access to gifted and special education programs?

When these questions are used to improve the quality of data collected, schools can effectively apply the lessons of self-reflection to the problems they recognize within their district as policy action. Ultimately, in a school context, it is the quality of teaching in each classroom that determines whether Hispanic/Latino students will move forward in their learning and achievement. Even in isolation, the efforts of effective teachers are relevant and meaningful, and students benefit from the structured opportunities these teachers provide. However, when the teacher is part of a larger comprehensive and programmatic infrastructure with multiple levels of support, the opportunities to develop and maximize student achievement are heightened. Every level of the school district should be an active participant every day. This is especially necessary when the district serves Hispanic/Latino students and other low-income, racially, culturally, and linguistically diverse students.

Actions need to be specifically geared toward increasing inclusivity and building a culture of achievement. In her article "Five Ways to Support Diverse Families," McKibben (2016) asserts that because American families are changing, schools must learn to adapt so they can create a more inclusive school community. She identified five strategies to help support diverse families:

1. **Dispel assumptions**—Unraveling assumptions requires educators to examine their default view of families.

2. **Reevaluate programs**—As a staff, examine how your existing programs accommodate—or turn away—different families.

3. **Use inclusive language**—Translate enrollment forms, permission slips, and other kinds of communication into students' home languages.

4. **Send a visible message of acceptance**—Signage in Spanish is posted and the Welcoming Schools starter kit recommends hosting a panel of parents from diverse backgrounds to talk about differences.

5. **Just listen and ask**—Active listening is safe and often a good starting point for connecting with families who are racially, culturally, and linguistically diverse.

On a districtwide level, action needs to include all the relevant stakeholders. Table 4.4 summarizes the key roles of the school board, superintendent, and principal, in addition to the role of teacher, which we have discussed in depth. The illustration of the continuum references the connectivity of the support services that align systemic infrastructure efforts.

**Table 4.4: Continuum of Support Services for Hispanic/Latino Students**

State Departments of Education — Local Boards of Education — Superintendents — District Office Specialists — Principals — Teachers — Parents/Family — Local Community

| | |
|---|---|
| **State Departments of Education** | Must actively recruit individuals who possess the expertise to guide and assist local districts in implementing comprehensive school reform that identifies services and supports for Hispanic/Latino students. |
| **Local Boards of Education** | Develop policies directed at Hispanic/Latino students that serve as accountability measures, ensuring their unique needs will be met. |
| **Superintendents** | Responsible for the day-to-day operations with influence to direct financial, programmatic, and human resources that impact Hispanic/Latino students. |
| **District Office Specialists** | Ensure that the on-the-ground support addresses principles of equity and access and assesses how their impact affects Hispanic/Latino students. |
| **Principals** | Hold high expectations of all stakeholder groups affecting Hispanic/Latino students and understand that they are foundational to building capacity and programmatic success. |
| **Teachers** | Plan and implement experiences and culturally responsive pedagogy that allow Hispanic/Latino students to grow academically, cognitively, socially, and emotionally. |
| **Parents/Family** | Collaborate with teachers and principals to ensure their child is equipped with the tools required to be active and engaged in the teaching and learning process. |
| **Local Community** | Partners with parents, schools, and/or the school district by offering programs and services that support the continuing education of Hispanic/Latino students. |

*The School Board*

The Center for Public Education (2016) writes that a local school board is a critical public link to public schools, and whether elected or appointed, school board members serve their communities in the following important ways.

- First and foremost, school boards look out for students. Education is not a line item on the school board's agenda—it is the only item.

- When making decisions about school programs, school boards incorporate their community's view of what students should know and be able to do.

- School boards are accessible to the public and accountable for the performance of their schools.

- School boards are the education watchdog for their communities, ensuring that students get the best education for the tax dollars spent.

One of the primary purposes of the National Hispanic Council of School Board Members (2016) is to promote and advance equal education opportunities for Hispanic children by council members becoming actively engaged in national dialogue on education problems, issues, and concerns in conjunction with the National School Boards Association and other national organizations committed to the continued growth and development of minority children.

*The Superintendent*

In a district's efforts to plan for the education of its Hispanic/Latino students, the superintendent finds him- or herself as the intermediary between the district's board of education and the programs implemented at the school level. The superintendent functions as the administrative manager of the district.

The Association of Latino Administrators and Superintendents (ALAS) (2016) has as its mission and primary focus leadership at the national level that ensures every school in America effectively serves the educational needs of all students with an emphasis on Latino youth by building capacity, promoting best practices, and transforming education institutions. ALAS is also committed to identifying, recruiting, developing, and advancing Latino school administrators in order to improve the education accomplishments of Latino youth.

Superintendents have a direct hand in how a school district addresses the education of its Hispanic/Latino students. As such, they are responsible for the day-to-day operations with influence to direct financial, programmatic, and human resources to this group of students. ALAS has on its website (alasedu.org/resources/white-papers) a list of white papers and other resources that can help school and district leaders with improving their level of understanding of Hispanic/Latino students and how to meet their education needs through the implementation of research and practice.

Policymaking occurs at the district's governing board level. The role of the super-intendent is to implement procedures to carry out the requirements of policy. These individuals also engage principals and teachers with implementation of research and practice and are held accountable by monitoring and assisting with compliance-re-lated expectations. Superintendents provide the on-the-ground support needed by principals and teachers. It is at this district office level where educational and instruc-tional leaders ensure that the support addresses principles of equity and access and how their impact affects Hispanic/Latino students. This is done by disaggregating data, monitoring the progress of district goals and objectives, and reporting trends in academic achievement.

### The Principal

At the school level, the buck stops with the principal. The principal's primary re-sponsibility is twofold: to ensure the life-safety and well-being of the school's students and to serve as the school's instructional leader. Both characteristics are consistent with the role of a principal who advances the education of the whole child. A well-in-formed school must also be able to identify the demographics of the community being served.

With reference to Hispanic/Latino students, it would behoove principals to know which of the twenty ethnicities are enrolled in their schools. This level of acknowledg-ment and understanding helps inform culturally responsive pedagogy and cross-cul-tural communication and understanding. It also informs leadership style in how they approach students, parents, families, and the surrounding community. Due to changing political climates; budgetary constraints; pressure from local, state, and national interest groups; and increased student diversity, school principals, now, more than ever, are required to demonstrate how socioeconomic status, ethnic background, and school outcomes are all connected.

The role of the principal is essential for the academic achievement and success of all students and the school itself. There are myriad studies of the principal role that exem-plify certain behaviors and actions (fostering a positive learning climate, focusing on student progress, valuing gender equity and multicultural education, and promoting early identification of learning difficulties) that may influence student achievement. Castellano and Francis (2014) contend that principals are in a position to empower, advocate, implement, monitor, and evaluate progress. He or she can allocate funds and resources, promote professional growth opportunities, and invite stakeholders to be part of a team approach that develops programs, products, and services that support Hispanic/Latino students.

Figures 4.3, 4.4, 4.5, and 4.6 (pages 109–111) contain policy action worksheets that set a vision for educating Hispanic/Latino students, identify standards for educating them, promote measures that ensure quality, and evaluate progress being made in educating Hispanic/Latino students. Every stakeholder—from classroom teachers setting their goals for the year to superintendents deciding on district policy—should utilize a set of worksheets or rubrics that outline what problems exist, what actions to take, and who to involve. Writing out your goals in actionable steps is the best way to begin achieving them.

| | |
|---|---|
| Given the sheer number of Hispanic students enrolled in our nation's public schools, state and district boards have an opportunity to drive reform efforts in the education of these students through identifying issues facing state and/or local districts and developing an approach to address these challenges. Therefore, it is important from the beginning that state and/or district boards develop a vision and strategy for educating Hispanic/Latino students. This worksheet provides some initial questions state and/or district boards should consider asking and the information they need to gather to have a complete picture. | |

| Setting a Vision for Educating Hispanic/Latino Students | Questions to Ask When Considering Policy Action |
|---|---|
| | ▸ What challenges exist in educating Hispanic/Latino students in the state and/or district? Does the state or district have information from surveys or questionnaires that helps answer the question? |
| | ▸ What challenges does the state or district currently face in its efforts to educate Hispanic/Latino students? Also, what are the issues faced by teachers and administrators? |
| | ▸ Has the state and/or district board interacted with and received input from stakeholder groups (teachers, administrators, parents and families, students, and members of the community) to provide additional perspectives on the challenges surrounding the education of Hispanic/Latino students? |
| | ▸ Does the state or district board require any induction or mentoring support for teachers and administrators serving Hispanic/Latino students? |
| | ▸ Does the state or district collect information about what schools are doing to address issues in educating Hispanic/Latino students? |
| | ▸ What state or district supports are in place and made available for Hispanic/Latino students and the teachers and administrators serving them? |
| | ▸ How are teacher preparation programs, professional development opportunities, and teacher induction programs aligned to support teachers and administrators serving Hispanic/Latino students? |

**Figure 4.3: Worksheet 1—Setting a vision for educating Hispanic/Latino students.**

Standards are an important tool available to state and district boards of education. Moving forward, state and district boards need to provide schools with goals and expectations for educating Hispanic/Latino students so that all teachers and administrators receive the support they need to be effective. This policy worksheet provides some of the key considerations when crafting standards designed to assist teachers and administrators.

| Identifying Standards for Educating Hispanic/Latino Students | Questions to Ask When Considering Policy Action |
|---|---|
| | ▸ What challenges in educating Hispanic/Latino students does the state and/or district board want to address through program standards? |
| | ▸ Are there specific statewide or districtwide supports that teachers and administrators need to be successful in serving Hispanic/Latino students? |
| | ▸ What foundational, structural, and instructional standards should state and district boards consider in their efforts in educating Hispanic/Latino students? |
| | ▸ How do current state or district standards emphasize the education of Hispanic/Latino students and the role of comprehensive support for teachers and administrators? |
| | ▸ Is there noninstructional time set aside for teachers and administrators to interact with mentors and experts about educating Hispanic/Latino students? |
| | ▸ What role do local, state, and national experts have, if any, in the programs, products, and services used by teachers and administrators in educating Hispanic/Latino students to achieve the goals linked to the standards? |
| | ▸ How could effective completion of a teacher and administrator induction program help them demonstrate competency and growth in educating Hispanic/Latino students? |
| | ▸ How might the standards be used to communicate a vision for educating Hispanic/Latino students, identify research-based program elements, and hold states and districts accountable for implementing these elements? |

**Figure 4.4: Worksheet 2—Identifying standards for educating Hispanic/Latino students.**

Teachers and administrators are at the heart of quality programming that addresses the education of Hispanic/Latino students. Given their importance, teachers and administrators are a vital component of an overall comprehensive program. As such, training and professional development are key elements of ensuring that they have the skill, ability, and desire to serve Hispanic/Latino students.

| Teacher and Administrator Selection | Questions to Ask When Considering Policy Action |
|---|---|
| | ▸ What challenges do states and districts face when trying to innovate, train, and provide quality programs to teachers and administrators serving Hispanic/Latino students? |

**Figure 4.5: Worksheet 3—Ensuring quality for educating Hispanic/Latino students.**

|  | ▸ What skills do teachers and administrators need to support Hispanic/Latino students, and do state and district leadership identify these skills prior to selection and hiring?<br>▸ What are the benchmarks or progress indicators that make a teacher or administrator effective in serving Hispanic/Latino students?<br>▸ What requirements could be added to provide states and districts with additional information or perspective when selecting teachers and administrators to work directly with Hispanic/Latino students?<br>▸ What kinds of compensation and recognition exist for teachers and administrators to ensure that enough quality candidates apply to work directly with Hispanic/Latino students?<br>▸ What training do teachers and administrators receive in educating Hispanic/Latino students prior to the start of the school year?<br>▸ What support do teachers and administrators receive during the school year?<br>▸ What tools are available to teachers and administrators to assess progress in the related standards of the state or district?<br>▸ How do teachers and administrators serving Hispanic/Latino students integrate the work they do into their own learning and professional development? |
|--|--|

The overarching goals of program evaluations should be to assess the quality of programs involving Hispanic/Latino students and to inform discussions on improving such programs across the state or district. No program is perfect, and no program is without merit. An effective evaluation system for serving and educating Hispanic/Latino students ensures that programs at both ends of the quality spectrum can identify strengths and areas of improvement and have direction for how teachers and administrators can continuously improve their practice.

| Evaluating Progress in Educating Hispanic/Latino Students | **Questions to Ask When Considering Policy Action** |
|--|--|
|  | ▸ What should be the role of the state and district in evaluating teachers and administrators serving Hispanic/Latino students (e.g., defining major elements to include in the assessment, disseminating information about what states and districts are doing to assess progress)?<br>▸ How are various standards integrated into evaluations to ensure that all teachers and administrators demonstrate competency in these standards?<br>▸ Does the state or district collect outcome data on teacher and administrator evaluations and link the information back to training and professional development programs that target the education of Hispanic/Latino students?<br>▸ How do teacher and administrator evaluations inform and/or impact schoolwide improvement and reform efforts that target Hispanic/Latino students? |

**Figure 4.6: Worksheet 4—Evaluating progress in educating Hispanic/ Latino students.**

| | ▸ How do teacher and administrator evaluations account for school culture?<br>▸ What supports and follow-up are in place for teachers and administrators who receive unsatisfactory evaluations for their work with Hispanic/Latino students?<br>▸ What is the role of program standards in evaluating program implementation and outcomes? |
| --- | --- |

Building a culture of achievement, promoting academic capacity, and sustaining programs, products, and services for moving Hispanic/Latino students forward involves active communication, collaboration, and collegiality of key stakeholder groups—among them teachers, administrators, parents, family, and community. Table 4.5 identifies a framework for moving Hispanic/Latino students forward by identifying eleven focus areas for teachers and administrators to incorporate into their school's or district's professional growth plans. They include (1) high expectations, (2) internal and external support, (3) background knowledge (building on what students know), (4) student validation through cultural competence and integration, (5) making meaningful connections beyond the classroom, (6) advanced knowledge and understanding, (7) critical thinking and problem solving, (8) metacognitive communication, (9) quality of work, (10) student engagement, and (11) building resiliency and perseverance.

## Conclusion

It is well documented that, as a group, Hispanic/Latino students most likely attend Title I schools, are served by a preponderance of inexperienced teachers, and are underrepresented in programs serving gifted, advanced, and high-ability learners. Consequently, the teaching force and other instructional and educational leaders often struggle in meeting the academic, cognitive, social, and emotional needs of Hispanic/Latino students with varying language skills and abilities and who represent the nineteen different Spanish-speaking countries and one territory of the world.

Education is a progressive practice, meaning that as teachers and administrators there is always something new to learn. We cannot do what we have always done with respect to professional growth and development. When it comes to diversity and achievement, for example, the tremendous variation between and among cultural and ethnic groups, specifically Hispanic/Latino students, means that they cannot be treated by referring to a list of characteristics or traits. We must learn to be nimble, to pivot when the circumstances call for doing something different in how we educate the largest ethnic group found in our public schools. This is a challenge that must be honored if we are to move our Hispanic/Latino students forward. Through continued education and collaboration, we must forge ahead to close achievement gaps, to become more culturally competent, and to use teaching and learning processes that

**Table 4.5: A Framework for Moving Hispanic/Latino Students Forward**

| | Students | Teachers | Administrators | Family/Community |
|---|---|---|---|---|
| **High Expectations** | • Are actively engaged in personalized learning by setting specific individualized goals for themselves<br>• Arrive to class on time with the necessary materials and ready to learn | • Encourage, motivate, inspire, and expect the best from their students<br>• Hold students accountable for mastering academic content<br>• Hold themselves accountable for teaching content in interesting and meaningful ways<br>• Model appropriate behaviors | • Encourage, motivate, inspire, and expect the best from their faculty, staff, and students<br>• Develop incentive programs for students who meet or exceed specific individual academic goals<br>• Model appropriate behaviors | • Provide an environment conducive to learning by providing access to materials, resources, and experiences<br>• Provide encouragement, motivation, and social/emotional support |
| **Internal and External Support** | • Actively engage in peer-peer mentoring programs and support groups in and/or out of school<br>• Ask for assistance related to their unique individual circumstances (academic, social, emotional) | • Engage in open and respectful communication<br>• Serve as resource persons and resource providers through teacher-student facilitation and mentoring<br>• Collaborate with other stakeholder groups to meet the needs of the whole child | • Engage in open and respectful communication<br>• Provide access and opportunity for students to participate in extracurricular activities that emphasize their strengths and/or interests | • Promote opportunities for students that instill a sense of pride and passion where they learn discipline toward something important to them<br>• Provide opportunities to participate in mentorships, apprenticeships, and sponsorships |
| **Background Knowledge: Building on What Students Know** | • Willingly share their personal experiences; make personal connections to the content being taught<br>• Engage their senses to help activate and/or identify knowledge | • Routinely incorporate the background knowledge of students into daily lessons across content<br>• Recognize and value student input | • Provide faculty and staff with the proper resources and training to identify strengths and weaknesses in the curriculum to help them fill the void | • Develop and promote partnerships and collaborations that promote the education of the whole child (academically, cognitively, socially, and emotionally) |

Continued →

| | Students | Teachers | Administrators | Family/Community |
|---|---|---|---|---|
| Student Validation Through Cultural Competence and Integration | ▸ Adhere to democratic principles of society<br>▸ Demonstrate both implicit and explicit knowledge of expectations from school, community, and society in general | ▸ Honor and respect the abilities of students<br>▸ Acknowledge their contributions on a daily basis<br>▸ Use culturally responsive pedagogy/practices<br>▸ Model culturally competent behaviors | ▸ Recognize student diversity and promote/display contributions of all groups through the use of symbolism (rituals, ceremonies, celebrations, branding of school) | ▸ Provide leadership opportunities that are significant and that allow students to influence an audience |
| Making Meaningful Connections Beyond the Classroom | ▸ Apply their knowledge, understanding, interests, strengths, and social networks beyond the classroom to demonstrate what they know and are able to do | ▸ Emphasize academic skills that promote lifelong learning<br>▸ Engage their students with opportunities in community-based service learning projects | ▸ Offer students academic-based experiences outside the traditional classroom<br>▸ Offer students flexible scheduling, if appropriate, to accommodate individual learning/academic goals | ▸ Offer students dual-enrollment opportunities<br>▸ Provide opportunities for student-led presentations to government officials, social service agencies, or other community-based groups |
| Advanced Knowledge and Understanding | ▸ Make deliberate choices to participate in academically rigorous course work<br>▸ Ask questions when they do not understand<br>▸ Complete course requirements demonstrating mastery of advanced knowledge and understanding | ▸ Participate in professional growth and development designed to enrich and/or accelerate learning (pace, complexity, depth)<br>▸ Model for students the application of advanced learning and understanding | ▸ Provide teaching faculty with professional development on culturally responsive pedagogy, cognitive rigor, and concept development<br>▸ Provide teaching faculty with the materials, supplies, and technology necessary to advance knowledge and understanding<br>▸ Offer students a continuum of services that include advanced academic programming | ▸ Demonstrate support for the value of an education through print media, social media, and tele/video communication<br>▸ Collaborate with and support the school district in its efforts to offer advanced academic programs (e.g., gifted education, honors programs, AP, and IB) |

| | Students | Teachers | Administrators | Family/Community |
|---|---|---|---|---|
| **Metacognitive Communication** | ▸ Expected to explain answers, processes, and procedures<br>▸ Expected to share, describe, and engage in active feedback regarding their thinking and problem-solving strategies<br>▸ Expected to apply metacognitive communication skills across content | ▸ Model specific processes and procedures to their students<br>▸ Develop assignments and assessments designed to elicit metacognitive communication strategies<br>▸ Provide explicit feedback and reinforcement for a job well done<br>▸ Engage in self-reflection and self-assessment on how they are impacting student learning | ▸ Engage in self-reflection and self-assessment on how they are impacting student learning<br>▸ Use both quantitative and qualitative data as a source of reflection<br>▸ Engage others with specific expertise to help solve problems | ▸ Invite students to participate in community-based brainstorming and problem-solving opportunities<br>▸ Support schools and students through incentive-based programs<br>▸ Engage in self-reflection and self-assessment on how they are impacting student learning |
| **Critical Thinking and Problem Solving** | ▸ Engage in self-reflection and self-assessment of skill and ability<br>▸ Participate in advanced academic programs<br>▸ Demonstrate respect for the abilities of others<br>▸ Apply their advanced skills in alternative performance-based lessons, activities, and assessments/evaluations | ▸ Engage in self-reflection and self-assessment of skill and ability<br>▸ Select or design supplemental curriculum materials that emphasize analysis, synthesis, and evaluation of information and data<br>▸ Model the effective use of critical thinking and problem-solving skills<br>▸ Routinely provide students opportunities to demonstrate skills individually, through small-group or whole-class lessons and projects | ▸ Engage in self-reflection and self-assessment of skill and ability<br>▸ Model the effective use of critical thinking and problem-solving skills<br>▸ Provide the teaching faculty with the materials and supplies required to engage students in higher-order cognitive skill development<br>▸ Engage in professional development opportunities specific to school-based administrators working with diverse student populations | ▸ Model the effective use of critical thinking and problem-solving skills<br>▸ Provide students the opportunity to apply skills through problem-based learning projects<br>▸ Encourage students to participate in academic-type competitions |

Continued →

| | Students | Teachers | Administrators | Family/Community |
|---|---|---|---|---|
| Quality of Work | • Lead conferences summarizing their work and abilities to teachers, parents/guardians, and other stakeholder groups<br>• Develop a portfolio of their best work<br>• Demonstrate what they know and are able to do through alternative formats<br>• Participate in developing criteria of work across content areas | • Routinely use rubrics, with student feedback, to describe quality of work<br>• Quality-of-work criteria are directly connected to lessons and assignments<br>• Submit student work to local, state, and national competitions for recognition<br>• Develop a professional portfolio detailing their work with students | • Showcase student work and accomplishments throughout the school<br>• Provide the necessary resources enabling students to produce their best work<br>• Recognize teachers for their innovative and creative work<br>• Develop a schoolwide portfolio detailing the work and accomplishments of the school | • Showcase student work and accomplishments throughout the community<br>• Serve as sponsors, paying the expenses associated with participating in local, state, and national competitions<br>• Use media resources to highlight students for their work and accomplishments |
| Student Engagement | • Are focused on the specific task at hand<br>• Complete assignments to demonstrate mastery<br>• Ask teachers for assistance if needed | • Initiate interesting lessons that are interactive and motivate students<br>• Differentiate instruction based on student interests and skills so that all are successful<br>• Routinely engage in self-reflection about quality of instruction | • Routinely are in the classrooms; have visible presence throughout school<br>• Provide teaching faculty with professional development on how to engage diverse student populations<br>• Have knowledge of strengths and weaknesses of teaching staff | • Encourage and motivate students to attend class; demonstrate that attendance is important<br>• Provide additional assistance in the form of tutors |
| Resiliency and Perseverance | • Get enough sleep<br>• Eat well<br>• Exercise<br>• Maintain positive relationships with adults<br>• Engage in problem-solving processes | • Promote positive social relationships with students<br>• Reinforce qualities that are key to resilience<br>• Avoid focusing on failure or negative behavior<br>• Share personal examples of resiliency and perseverance | • Apply restorative justice techniques and strategies<br>• Share personal examples of resiliency and perseverance<br>• Provide extra support to teachers, such as training, time to unwind | • Display stability and support and emphasize high expectations<br>• Serve as, or provide access to, a caring adult outside the family<br>• Foster feelings of competence and worth |

inspire, motivate, and engage students at higher levels of achievement. As educators, we must become invested in our students socially and emotionally, learning more about them and applying pedagogy that makes a difference. Professional growth and development allow us to do that.

Through professional growth and development, we reflect on our own viewpoints and biases as a starting point. We must be willing participants and want to make a difference in the lives of the Hispanic/Latino students we serve. Teachers and administrators who accept this paradigm for professional learning put themselves in a position to be successful in educating low-income racially, culturally, and linguistically diverse students. Those who continue to rely on conventional wisdom and the status quo are part of a failing process that perpetuates the standing of Hispanic/Latino students as one of the lowest-achieving groups in the United States. The purpose of this chapter is to identify practices that enable teachers and administrators to become more culturally competent and effective instructional leaders to support Hispanic/Latino students.

They are in a position to revisit curriculum and instruction and infuse meaningful learning experiences that address multiple perspectives that help students move to a deeper knowledge of personal validation by emphasizing cross-cultural communication and understanding, acceptance, and the celebration of diversity. However, before they can do this with their Hispanic/Latino students, they must first engage themselves in a process of self-reflection and self-assessment of how they perceive others who are different from themselves. This self-examination will help them gain a clearer understanding of their own experiences, boundaries, and challenges and further provides them with a platform that helps bridge relational and instructional pedagogy through professional learning in multicultural education and cultural competency.

# Final Thoughts

## Ethan's Story

At first glance, Ethan appeared to be very serious and reserved in his appearance and demeanor. His mother and stepfather assured me that, for the most part, he is just the opposite. They view him as a loving, caring son who is "an all-American next-door type of kid." He plays with toys, has best friends, is into Pokémon, enjoys time with his cousins, participates in martial arts, and does exceptionally well in school.

Of Puerto Rican and Mexican descent, Ethan is seven years old and will be entering a gifted second-grade class in the fall of 2017 in his local public school. His academic excellence and joy for learning has been validated by his parents, teachers, and building principal. His multiple academic achievements have placed him on the Principal's Honor Roll on multiple occasions. This level of academic excellence is atypical of Mexican and Puerto Rican students who, the research purports, are two of the most poverty-stricken and lowest achieving of all students of Hispanic ethnicity.

When asked how he feels about school, he responded, "School is fun. I have my group of friends, and I enjoy learning what my teachers teach. I think I do so well in school because my teachers make learning fun." To the question about which teachers are his favorites, and why, Ethan states, "My media teachers, Ms. Barrera and Ms. Ornstein, because they engage us in hands-on projects and capitalize on our interests. They ask us what we want to learn and create projects for us to complete." The research and practice on teaching gifted, advanced, and high-ability students confirm that these teaching and learning processes are particularly effective. "I like all my teachers." He claims they are all cool and make learning fun. When I asked if there was anything he wanted his teachers to know about him, he hesitated a bit. Eventually, he said, "I wished my teachers knew that I liked to sing and dance."

Ethan is a voracious reader, partly because he enjoys reading and partly because his mom and stepdad require him to read every day. At times, this has been a point of contention between them. His mother, Adelaida, insists that reading is fundamental to success and important for his future and will not waiver from her position. Ethan wishes his parents would give him a break every now and then.

During our interview, Ethan did open up a bit more, feeling more relaxed. When I asked who inspires and motivates him, he quickly responded, "My parents and Ms. Tressel, my math teacher. I do like all of my teachers, but she tells me that math is a tool that will help me become a better critical thinker and problem solver." As for his friends, he did say that he has three close friends at school. He further added that, "They are my best friends because they are always by my side. Together we stand up against bullies, and we also enjoy pranking one another."

As our meeting was coming to an end, I asked, "If you could have lunch with any-one in the world, anyone in history, who would it be, and why?" Without hesitation, he named Abraham Lincoln. "Abraham Lincoln was a great man who did a lot for humanity. I admire him very much." I was impressed by this seven-year-old's selec-tion. When I asked him if he could change one thing about the world, what would it be and why, he responded, "I would not let evil take over the world." This sense of goodness and justice is typical of gifted students; nonetheless, his response displayed a sense of maturity not often associated with children his age.

My final query to Ethan was about his future. "Well, I am thinking about joining the army to be a K-9 [canine] officer. I do know I want to work with dogs. They're amazing creatures." I left the interview feeling impressed with Ethan. It is very clear that his parents have his best interests in mind and support him in any way they can. They make sure he participates in a vast array of enrichment activities. After our meeting, the family was headed out to take an art class together based on their live observations of manatees. With their continued love and support, I do not doubt for a minute that Ethan has a bright future and will be successful in any career to which he sets his mind.

## Justin's Story

Justin is thirteen years old and will be entering the eighth grade in the fall of 2017. (As of this writing, Justin is really twelve years old. However, he insisted that I write he is thirteen because his birthday is just two months away.) Nilsa, his mother, is Puerto Rican, and his father is Cuban. He lives in a single-parent family, with his mother and grandmother in a Hispanic barrio where speaking Spanish is the norm. Justin is a smart boy but does not want his friends to know. But it's OK that they know he plays both the trumpet and baritone in the school band. He ended seventh grade with straight As in all core academic classes, of which one was advanced/honors math. He was one of four Hispanic boys in his advanced math class of thirty students. He made the Principal's List and Honor Roll for his academic accomplishments.

As I interviewed Justin during lunch, I asked why he didn't want his friends from school and his neighborhood to know that he was a smart, intelligent young man. His response was very consistent with that of other smart boys of color. "I don't want people to know how I act in class and what I say, how I perform. I want them to think I am cool. I'm not a nerd." When I inquired if he would consider enrolling in all advanced/honors courses in eighth grade, he scoffed and said, "There is too much pressure being in advanced and honors classes. Why would I want pressure when I know I can do very well in just regular classes?" I did remind him that his mother would be reading this interview.

In between bites of pizza, I asked Justin about his middle school teachers and if he had any favorites and why. Without hesitation, he mentioned two names, Ms. Russell and Ms. Faust. "Ms. Faust actually teaches. She does not get mad, nor does she yell or scream. She gives us individual assistance when needed. And Ms. Faust doesn't play! She is strict and knows how to keep me focused without being mean about it." As a follow-up, I asked him what he would like teachers to know about him. After some contemplation, he responded, "Well, I'm a pretty open book. However, I would want them to know that they need to be strict with me, though I would never tell them."

As our lunch hour was winding down, I inquired about his family and friends, his closest friends. Justin told me that he has two very close friends (one boy, one girl). When I asked what makes a good friend, a best buddy, he responded, "My two best friends are there for me. I trust them, and they trust me. We talk about everything. If we have a disagreement, we talk it out." During our time together, it was very clear that Justin loves his family. He has an absentee father but stated, "He is a good guy for the most part, and I love him." He went on to say, "My mother is everything to me, and I love her very much. Along with my godmother and younger stepsisters, they are my biggest influences, and they inspire me to be the best I can be. I want to do well for them."

My last question to Justin was about how he saw his future. "My future is looking good; it's bright." He said that he and his mom were currently at odds about where he should go to high school. She wants him to pursue his music at the renowned high school of the arts. He wants to go to his neighborhood high school but still wants to join the school's music/band program, though it's a small program. It is better known for its IB and environmental sciences magnet programs. Time will tell how this plays out.

In reflecting on this interview, it is clear that Justin has the support of his mother and extended family. He is a smart, intelligent, vibrant young man filled with talent and potential. I have encouraged his mother to think about enrolling him in all honors/advanced classes during his eighth-grade year. It is important that he be exposed to others who are his intellectual peers. It is important that he be challenged academically and given the social and emotional support that helps him understand that being Hispanic and smart is OK. It is important because as a nation we are allowing Hispanic young men like Justin to fall between the cracks, not realizing what they have to offer. Local, state, and national achievement data bear this out. Justin's future offers unlimited possibilities.

## The Power of Communication and Collaboration

Fast-forward three months: Ethan is excelling in his second-grade gifted class, and Justin's mother, Nilsa, did, in fact, enroll him in all honors classes for his eighth-grade year. Justin has claimed that he has never had to work so hard before in school. Nilsa says that he does complain about the work but completes all his assignments. Nilsa and Ethan's mother, Adelaida, work together at a child development center. They rely on each other for support in dealing with two precocious boys and in navigating the complexities of honors education. Often, they schedule their parent-teacher conferences for the same night so they can go together. There are times when both boys visit at the same time, mostly after school. I have spoken to them on these occasions, and they both appear to be happy and content, Ethan more so than Justin, who misses his regular education friends, but is working to connect with his new classmates.

I have the highest hopes for both their futures.

## The Haves and Have-Nots

Castellano (2011) asserts that every large urban environment is a tale of two cities that is comprised, in part, of the haves and have-nots. The public schools of these environments are a reflection of the greater society that exists and serve as the reality for its citizens. Here is an example. In the Miami-Dade County School District, one of the ten largest public school districts in the United States, there are communities primarily inhabited by the wealthy, privileged, and/or well educated. The children of these families attend schools of excellence where the expectations are high, achievement is expected, the curriculum is taught by experienced and credentialed instructional staff members with advanced degrees, and the involvement of the parents in the education of their children is clearly evident.

In the same district, there are other communities where poverty, despair, and feelings of isolation are the norm. Related characteristics of these environments may include a high incidence of gang involvement and violence, drug use, domestic violence, single-parent families, teenage pregnancy, undocumented groups, and a citizenship that is culturally, ethnically, linguistically, and racially diverse. The children of these families attend schools in older facilities where most qualify for free or reduced-price lunch, are eligible to receive Title I services, have an inexperienced teaching staff, and are provided older and fewer resources to supplement the curricular programs of their schools. In these communities, involving the parents in the education of their children is challenging and often frustrating.

The disparity within these districts isn't the fault of the students. The responsibility falls on the stakeholder groups: parents and families, the school, the school district, and the local community. The unclaimed talent and potential of Hispanic/Latino students is confounding at best. By far the largest ethnic group to attend the nation's public schools, these students continue to be one of the lowest achieving of all sub-groups. Moreover, of the 12.5 million Hispanic students that represent twenty different ethnicities, approximately 3.8 million of this group are also identified as ELLs and another 840,000 identified as special needs (National Center for Educational Statistics, 2016a). In a nation where education is a fundamental right, the challenges for educating this complex intra-ethnic diverse group of students are immense. Like for all others, Hispanic/Latino students deserve a system of education that is inclusive; promotes equity, access, and opportunity; and supports excellence using curriculum, instruction, and assessment strategies that are not only rigorous and relevant but also differentiated and culturally responsive and account for reaching and teaching the whole child. If that's a mouthful to read out loud, it's infinitely more overwhelming to implement in nationwide policy.

Educating Hispanic/Latino students is a bottom-up movement, not top-down. It's a game of advocacy: The needs of Hispanic/Latino students are advocated for first by the teachers who work with them daily in their schools. Schools advocate on the teachers' behalf to the district. The district advocates on the school's behalf to the state. And the state can advocate for their districts at the federal level. Reaching the most influential policymakers begins with teachers who take it upon themselves to become informed and engaged with who their students are and what they need.

Public schools in the United States should truly embrace the construct of "public." All students should be welcomed, supported, and allowed to achieve to their greatest potential through the principles of equity, access, and opportunity. Hispanic/Latino students are the largest ethnic group found in our schools today. As such, schools should be responsive to their needs as they prepare them for a democratic society. Poverty should not define this group of students. English language proficiency should not define these students. The toxic stress that many endure should not define them. And neither should immigration status. Throughout this book, we have offered a plethora of research and data, strategies and techniques, and a foundation for how to build and sustain capacity in how we educate this complex cross section of students. They deserve the best we have to offer. Our focus should be on what schools can and should provide for all students.

Hispanic/Latino students need support in dealing with the trauma of entering this country illegally. They need resources devoted to offsetting the effects of poverty. They need informed educators to help them navigate and understand their complicated personal identity. We can help them by acknowledging the influence of these struggles on academic performance, by investing the time to constantly improve our profession, by being responsive and proactive to their best learning strategies, by addressing the disparity in gifted and special education representation, and by raising both our expectations of how much these students can achieve and how little we ask them to show us. When teachers choose to make a difference in the lives of Hispanic/Latino students, they are increasing the chance of success for generations of learners—and it is a choice. Are you the type of educator who chooses to continue teaching as you always have, or are you the type who chooses to make a difference?

# References and Resources

ACT and Excelencia in Education. (2016). *The condition of college and career readiness 2015: Hispanic students.* Iowa City, IA: Author.

Annie E. Casey Foundation. (2016). *KIDS COUNT data book: State trends in child well-being.* Baltimore, MD: Author.

Association of Latino Administrators and Superintendents. (2016). *Welcome to ALAS.* Retrieved from alasedu.org.

Banks, J. A. (2008). Diversity, group identity, and citizenship education in a global age. *Educational Researcher, 37*(3), 19–139.

Baylor, E. (2016). *Closed doors: Black and Latino students are excluded from top research universities.* Center for American Progress. Retrieved from www.americanprogress.org/issues/education/reports/2016/10/13/145098/closed-doors-black-and-latino-students-are-excluded-from-top-public-universities

Bhattacharjee, Y. (2012). *Why bilinguals are smarter.* Retrieved from www.google.com/search?q=why+bilinguals+are+smarter+yudhijit+bhattacharjee&rlz=1C1CHFX_venUS571US572&oq=Why+Bilinguals+&aqs=chrome.2.0j69i57j0l4.5774j0j4&sourceid=chrome&ie=UTF-8

Boschma, J., & Brownstein, R. (2016). The concentration of poverty in American schools. *Atlantic.* Retrieved from www.theatlantic.com/education/archive/2016/02/concentration-poverty-american-schools/471414/

Brophy, J. E. (1983). Research on the self-fulfilling prophecy and teacher expectations. *Journal of Educational Psychology, 75*(5), 631–661.

Burnett, J. (2017). He crossed the border in a packed, unventilated trailer and survived. *NPR.* Retrieved from www.npr.org/2017/08/17/543723961/he-crossed-the-border-in-a-packed-unventilated-trailer-and-survived

Camera, L. (2016). Gains in reading for Hispanic students overshadowed by achievement gap. *U.S. News and World Report*. Retrieved from www.usnews.com/news/blogs /data-mine/2016/03/28/hispanic-students-gains-overshadowed-by-achievement-gaps

Castellano, J. A. (2003). *Special populations in gifted education: Working with diverse gifted learners.* Boston, MA: Allyn and Bacon.

Castellano, J. A. (2004). Empowering and serving Hispanic students in gifted education. In D. Boothe & J. C. Stanley (Eds.), *In the eyes of the beholder: Critical issues for diversity in gifted education* (pp. 1–14). Waco, TX: Prufrock Press.

Castellano, J. A. (2011). Cultural competency: Implications for educational and instructional leaders in gifted education. In J. A. Castellano & A. D. Frazier (Eds.), *Special populations in gifted education: Understanding our most able students from diverse backgrounds* (pp. 383–400). Waco, TX: Prufrock Press.

Castellano, J. A. (2011). Hispanic students and gifted education: New outlooks, perspectives, and paradigms. In J. A. Castellano & A. D. Frazier (Eds.), *Special populations in gifted education: Understanding our most able students from diverse backgrounds* (pp. 249–272). Waco, TX: PrufrockPress.

Castellano, J. (2016). Si se puede / Yes we can: Ramping up efforts for collaborating with Hispanic parents and families. In J. L. Davis & J. L. Moore III (Eds.), *Gifted children of color from around the world: Exemplary practices and directions for the future* (pp. 37–52). United Kingdom: Emerald Press.

Castellano, J. A., & Diaz, E. I. (2002). *Reaching new horizons: Gifted and talented education for culturally and linguistically diverse students.* Boston, MA: Allyn and Bacon.

Castellano, J. A., & Francis, E. M. (2014). Working within the system to build effective policies and practices. In M. S. Matthews & J. A. Castellano (Eds.), *Talent development for English language learners: Identifying and developing potential* (pp. 191–216). Waco, TX: Prufrock Press.

Castellano, J. A., & Matthews, M. S. (2014). Legal issues in gifted education. In J. P. Bakken, F. E. Obiakor, & A. F. Rotatori (Eds.), *Gifted education: Current perspectives and issues* (pp. 1–20). United Kingdom: Emerald Group Publishing Limited.

Ceci, S. J., & Williams, W. M. (1997). Schooling, intelligence, and income. *American Psychologist, 52,* 1051–1058.

Center for Public Education. (2016). *The role of school boards.* Retrieved from www.center forpubliceducation.org/You-May-Also-Be-Interested-In-landing-page-level/Audience -The-Public-YMABI/The-Role-of-School-Boards

Child Trends. (2016). *Moving beyond trauma: Child migrants and refugees in the United States.* Bethesda, MD: Author.

Child Trends Data Bank. (2016). *Educational attainment: Indicators on children and youth.* Bethesda, MD: Author.

Child Trends Hispanic Institute. (2014). *America's Hispanic children: Gaining ground, looking forward*. Bethesda, MD: Author.

Child Trends Hispanic Institute. (2016). *The invisible ones: How Latino children are left out of our nation's census count*. Bethesda, MD: Author.

Child Trends Hispanic Institute. (2017). *Making math count more for young Latino children*. Bethesda, MD: Author.

Clark, B. (2013). *Growing up gifted* (8th ed.). Upper Saddle River, NJ: Pearson.

Colangelo, N., Assouline, S. G., Marron, M. A., Castellano, J. A., Clinkenbeard, P. R., Rogers, K., Calvert, E., Malek, R., & Smith, D. (2010). Guidelines for developing an academic acceleration policy. *Journal of Advanced Academics, 21*(2), 180–203.

Condition of Latinos in Education. (2015). *2015 factbook*. Washington, DC: Author.

Darity, W. (2016). *The Latino flight to whiteness*. Retrieved from http://prospect.org /article/latino-flight-whiteness

Darity, W., Dietrich, J., & Hamilton, D. (2005). Bleach in the rainbow: Latin ethnicity and preference for whiteness. *Transforming Anthropology, 13*(2), 103–109.

Davis, J. L. (2012). The importance of family engagement. In M. R. Coleman & S. K. Johnsen (Eds.), *Implementing RTI with gifted students: Service models, trends, and issues* (pp. 47–65). Waco, TX: Prufrock Press.

Deruy, E. (2016). How perceptions about opportunity vary by race. *Atlantic*. Retrieved from www.theatlantic.com/education/archive/2016/03/americans-different -perceptions-of-opportunity/473127/

Duncan, A. (2015). *A set of rights to help parents seek high quality education for their children*. A paper presented at the 2015 National Parent Teacher Association Convention and Expo, Charlotte, NC.

Ford, D. Y. (2014, Fall). Desegregating gifted education for underrepresented students: Equity promotes equality. *Teaching for High Potential*, 1, 16–18.

Franklin, J. (2008). *Research brief for schools: Social and emotional learning: The foundation of student success in school, work, and life*. Retrieved from http://web.extension.illinois .edu/sel/pdf/sel_research_brief_for_schools_2008-04-15.pdf

French, D. (2016). Disrupting inequity. *ASCD Express, 12*(6), 1–3.

Friend, M., & Bursuck, W. D. (2015). *Including students with special needs: A practical guide for classroom teachers* (7th ed.). Boston, MA: Pearson.

Gandara, P. (2005). *Fragile futures: Risk and vulnerability among Latino high achievers*. Princeton, NJ: Educational Testing Service.

Gentry, M., & Mann, R. (2008). *Total school cluster grouping and differentiation: A comprehensive, research-based plan for raising student achievement and improving teacher practices*. Mansfield Center, CT: Creative Learning Press.

Gill, S., Posamentier, J., & Hill, P. T. (2016). *Suburban schools: The unrecognized frontier in public education.* Seattle, WA: Center for Reinventing Public Education.

Horak, A. K., Holincheck, N., Webb, K., & Nagy, S. (2017, May). *Empowering English language learners' academic potential through problem-based learning: Leading teachers with a lens for capacity.* Paper presented at American Educational Research Association, San Antonio, TX.

Institute for Educational Leadership. (2005). *Preparing and supporting diverse culturally competent leaders: Practice and policy considerations.* Washington, DC: Author.

Institute for Educational Leadership. (2011). *State education agencies as agents of change: What will it take for the states to step up on education reform?* Washington, DC: Author.

Kirp, T. (2006). After the bell curve. *New York Times,* p. C6.

Kneebone, E., & Berube, A. (2013). *Confronting suburban poverty in America.* Washington, DC: Brookings Institute.

Lucille Packard Foundation for Children's Health. (2015). *Public school enrollment, by race/ethnicity.* Retrieved from www.kidsdata.org/topic/36/publicschoolenrollment-race/table#fmt=451&loc=1&tf=84&ch=7,11,621,85,10,72,9,73&sortColumnId=0&sortType=asc

Marian, V., & Shook, A. (2012). *The cognitive benefits of being bilingual.* Retrieved from http://dana.org/Cerebrum/2012/The_Cognitive_Benefits_of_Being_Bilingual/

Matthews, M. S., & Castellano, J. A. (2014). *Talent development of English language learners: Identifying and developing potential.* Waco, TX: PrufrockPress.

Matthews, M. S., & Castellano, J. A. (2014). Thoughts for the future. In M. S. Matthews & J. A. Castellano (Eds.), *Talent development of English language learners: Identifying and developing potential* (pp. 217–228). Waco, TX: PrufrockPress.

Matthews, P. H. (2014). Using service learning to support high-ability English language learners. In M. S. Matthews & J. A. Castellano (Eds.), *Talent development of English language learners: Identifying and developing potential* (pp. 167–190). Waco, TX: PrufrockPress.

Mckibbon, S. (2015). Five ways to support diverse families. *Education Update, 27*(5). Alexandria, VA: ASCD.

Migration Policy Institute. (2015a). *States and districts with the highest number and share of English language learners.* Washington, DC: Author.

Migration Policy Institute. (2015b). *Top languages spoken by English language learners nationally and by state.* Washington, DC: Author.

Mitchell, C. (2016). Bungling student names: A slight that stings. *Education Week, 35*(30), 1, 10–11.

Mitchell, C. (2016). Nearly half of U.S. states offer special recognition of bilingual graduates. *Education Week*. Retrieved from http://blogs.edweek.org/edweek/learning-the-language/2016/09/nearly_half_of_us_states_recog.html

Moore III, J. L., Ford, D. Y., & Milner, H. R. (2005b). Underachievement among gifted students of color: Implications for educators. *Theory into Practice, 44*(2), 167–177.

Murphey, D., Guzman, L., & Torres, A. (2014). *America's Hispanic children: Gaining ground, looking forward*. Bethesda, MD: Child Trends Hispanic Institute.

National Assessment of Educational Progress. (2016). *Nation's report card*. Retrieved from https://nces.ed.gov/nationsreportcard/

National Association for Gifted Children. (2016). *Parent and community network position statement*. Washington, DC: Author.

National Association of State Boards of Education. (2016). *Education issues*. Retrieved from www.nasbe.org.

National Center for Educational Statistics. (2016a). *Back to school statistics for 2016*. Retrieved from https://nces.ed.gov/fastfacts/display.asp?id=372

National Center for Educational Statistics. (2016b). *Preschool and kindergarten enrollment*. Retrieved from https://nces.ed.gov/programs/coe/indicator_cfa.asp

National Education Association. (2013). *Early childhood education*. Retrieved from www.nea.org/home/18163.htm

National Hispanic Council of School Board Members. (2016). NHC works to support the educational achievement of Hispanic students. Retrieved from www.nsba.org/services/caucuses/national-hispanic-caucus-school-board-members/bylaws

National Research Center on Hispanic Children and Families. (2016). *A national portrait of the health and education of Hispanic boys and young men*. Bethesda, MD: Author.

National Science Board. (2010). *Preparing the next generation of STEM innovators: Identifying and developing our nation's human capital* (NSB-10-33). Washington, DC: National Science Board.

Network for Public Education. (2016). *Valuing public education: A 50 state report card*. Key Gardens, NY: Author.

O'Conner, C., & Deluca-Fernandez, S. (2006). Race, class, and disproportionality: Reevaluating the relationship between poverty and special education placement. *Educational Researcher, 35*(6), 6–11.

Okeeheelee Middle School. (2017). Students at Okeeheelee Middle School Take, Pass College-Level Advanced Placement Test. Retrieved from www.okeeheelee.org/tag/ap-exam/

Olszewski-Kubilius, P., & Clarenbach, J. (2012). *Unlocking emerging talent: Supporting high achievement of low-income, high-ability students*. Washington, DC: National Association for Gifted Children.

Pew Research Center: Hispanic Trends. (2012a). *Hispanic student enrollments reach new highs in 2011*. Washington, DC: Author.

Pew Research Center: Hispanic Trends. (2012b). *When labels don't fit: Hispanics and their views on identity*. Washington, DC: Author.

Pew Research Center: Hispanic Trends. (2016). *U.S. Latino population growth and dispersion has slowed since the onset of the great recession*. Washington, DC: Author.

Plucker, J., Giancola, J., Healy, G., Arndt, D., & Wang, W. (2015). *Equal talents, unequal opportunities: A report card on state support for academically talented low-income students*. Lansdown, VA: Jack Kent Cooke Foundation.

Rapaport, L. (2017). *Preteens who mistrust teachers less likely to reach college*. Retrieved from www.reuters.com/article/us-health-adolescents-teacher-trust-idUSKBN15N2K7

Rix, K. (2010, May). ELL in the heartland. *Scholastic Administrator*, 6–8.

Roberts, S. (2016). Hispanic surnames on the rise in U.S. as immigration surges. *New York Times*. Retrieved from www.nytimes.com/2016/12/15/us/census-data-hispanic-surnames.html

Samuels, C. A. (2016a). In special education: A debate on bias. *Education Week, 35*(32), 1, 17.

Samuels, C. A. (2016b). *Final rule released on identifying racial bias in special education*. Retrieved from http://blogs.edweek.org/edweek/speced/2016/12/disproportionality_final_rule.html

Sanchez Zinny, G. (2012). Hispanic achievement: Not only a matter of education. *Huffington Post*. Retrieved from www.huffingtonpost.com/gabriel-sanchez-zinny/hispanic-students-education_b_2051111.html

Sparks, S. D. (2016). Rich districts post widest racial gaps: Database sheds new light on achievement disparities. *Education Week, 35*(30), 1, 12–13.

Stepien, W. J., & Pyke, S. (1997). Designing problem-based learning units. *Journal for the Education of the Gifted, 20*, 380–400. https://doi.org/10.1177/016235329702000404

Turkheimer, E., Haley, A., D'Onofrio, B., Waldron, M., & Gottesman, I. I. (2003). Socioeconomic status modifies heritability of IQ in young children. *Psychological Science, 14*, 623–628.

United States Bureau of Labor Statistics. (2016). *Occupational employment statistics program: Employment, wages, and projected change in employment by typical entry-level education*. Washington, DC: Author.

United States Census Bureau. (2012). *Projected population by single year of age, sex, race, and Hispanic origin for the United States: 2012–2060*. Washington, DC: Author.

United States Census Bureau. (2013). Poverty rates for selected detailed race and Hispanic groups by state and place: 2007–2011. *American Community Survey Briefs*. Washington, DC: Author.

United States Census Bureau. (2014). *Race reporting among Hispanics: 2010.* Washington, DC: Author.

United States Census Bureau. (2016). *Table 1: Educational attainment of the population 18 years and over, by age, sex, race, and Hispanic origin.* Washington, DC: Author.

United States Department of Education. (2010). *Status and trends in the education of racial and ethnic groups.* Washington, DC: Author.

United States Department of Education. (2016). *The state of racial diversity in the educator workforce.* Washington, DC: Author.

United States Department of Education, National Center for Educational Statistics. (2013). Table 209.10: Number and percentage of distribution of teachers in public and private elementary and secondary schools, by selected teacher characteristics: Selected years, 1987–1988 through 2011–2012. *Digest of Educational Statistics.* Washington, DC: Author.

United States Department of Education, National Center for Educational Statistics. (2014). Table 204.50. Children 3 to 21 years old served under Individual with Disabilities Education Act (IDEA), Part B, by Race/Ethnicity and Type of Disability: 2011–2012 and 2012–2013. *Digest of Educational Statistics.* Washington, DC: Author.

United States Department of Education, Office for Civil Rights. (2016). *Securing equal educational opportunity: Report to the president and secretary of education.* Washington, DC: Author.

United States Government Accountability Office. (2016). *K–12 education: Better use of information could help agencies identify disparities and address racial discrimination.* Washington, DC: Author.

Western Interstate Commission for Higher Education. (2012). *Knocking at the college door: Projections of high school graduates by state and race/ethnicity.* Boulder, CO: Author.

White, W. (2002). *The gifted curriculum.* Unpublished manuscript.

Williams Institute. (2014). *LGBT and same sex couple demographics in the US.* Retrieved from http://williamsinstitute.law.ucla.edu/press/in-the-news/interactive-lgbt-and-same -sex-couple-demographics/

Winebrenner, S. (2001). *Teaching gifted kids in the regular classroom: Strategies and techniques every teacher can use to meet the academic needs of the gifted and talented.* Minneapolis, MN: Free Spirit.

World Atlas. (2016). *US states with the largest relative Hispanic and Latino populations.* Retrieved from www.worldatlas.com/articles/us-states-with-the-largest-relative-hispanic-and-latino-populations.html